Rev!

MAGAZINE'S
BATHROOM
GUIDE TO
LEADERSHIP

Group

Loveland, Colorado
www.group.com

Group resources actually work!

This Group resource helps you focus on **"The 1 Thing®"**— a life-changing relationship with Jesus Christ. "The 1 Thing" incorporates our **R.E.A.L.** approach to ministry. It reinforces a growing friendship with Jesus, encourages long-term learning, and results in life transformation, because it's:

Relational
Learner-to-learner interaction enhances learning and builds Christian friendships.

Experiential
What learners experience through discussion and action sticks with them up to 9 times longer than what they simply hear or read.

Applicable
The aim of Christian education is to equip learners to be both hearers and doers of God's Word.

Learner-based
Learners understand and retain more when the learning process takes into consideration how they learn best.

REV! Magazine's Bathroom Guide to Leadership
Copyright © 2007 Group Publishing, Inc.

Visit our Web site: www.group.com

Credits
Editor: E. Paul Allen
Developer: Roxanne Wieman
Project Manager: Scott M. Kinner
Chief Creative Officer: Joani Schultz

Art Director: Jeff Storm
Cover Designer: The DesignWorks Group, Inc.
Interior Designer: The DesignWorks Group, Inc.
Production Manager: DeAnne Lear

Thanks to our talented authors!
Thomas Addington, Paul Allen, Charles Arn, Steve Ayers, Hans Finzel, Dave Fleming, Mike Foss, Stephen Graves, Robert Johnson, Tammy Kelley, Paul Krause, Scott Larsen, Ron Martoia, John Maxwell, Brian McClaren, David McQueen, Alan Nelson, Dean Ridings, Thom Schultz, Jeff Strong, Darren Walter, and Rick Warren

Library of Congress Cataloging-in-Publication Data
Rev! magazine's bathroom guide to leadership. — 1st American pbk. ed.
    p. cm.
  ISBN 978-0-7644-3568-3 (pbk. : alk. paper)
    1. Christian leadership. 2. Pastoral theology. I. Group Publishing.
II. Rev! magazine.
      BV652.1.R48 2007
      253—dc22   2007012338

10 9 8 7 6 5 4 3 2 1   16 15 14 13 12 11 10 09 08 07
Printed in the United States of America.

Rev!

MAGAZINE'S
BATHROOM
GUIDE TO
LEADERSHIP

TABLE OF CONTENTS

Let's face it...leadership leaks! (Pun intended.) And it's important that as leaders we're leaking the right stuff to those we're leading. Are we leading them with a servant's heart, living in a way that Jesus is seen living through us? Here at REV! we realize how important it is for pastors to have consistent, biblically sound, culturally relevant, and just plain ol' common sense information that encourages them to be the leader God's called them to be.

So we've scoured our issues of REV! and compiled this easy-to-read book on leadership. And like the name says, "REV! Magazine's Bathroom Guide to Leadership" we've provided it in a way that you can glean quick and challenging information and ideas on being a better leader—at home, at church, and in your community.

So, have fun flushing out (I've gotta stop) some great ideas that you can apply today as a leader...and take the plunge (OK, one more) into this our first of many bathroom guides.

PLUNGE INTO PERSONAL CHALLENGES

"Do you wish to rise? Begin by descending.
You plan a tower that will pierce the clouds?
Lay first the foundation of humility."

—ST. AUGUSTINE

(September/October 2004, pg.76)

A VIEW FROM THE BACK SEAT

by STEVE AYERS | *(September/October 2000)*

Back seats just weren't made for me.

I remember the days before air bags, when I was forced to share the back seat with my siblings as my father drove. It wasn't fun. Since then back seats have bored me—mainly because if I'm in the back seat, I'm not driving.

Yet I've learned in more than nine years of pastoring Hillvue Heights Church in Bowling Green, Kentucky, that "back-seat pastoring" is more effective than "front-seat pastoring." On March 10, 1991, my first Sunday as pastor of Hillvue Heights, I gave up driving and began to take a back seat in pastoring. I found that my plans, purposes, and understanding of the kingdom of God weren't what would power the church. I realized that loving Jesus is what powers the pastorate. Jesus doesn't need me to power the church. He loves me, and through this love, the pastorate has power.

Pastoring from the back-seat position, I've learned to love the church. It's always difficult for leaders to love the church when they believe the church will go awry if they take their hands off the steering wheel. When leaders believe their only job is to steer, it's hard to touch broken lives and allow themselves to become a healing agent of Christ. When God called me to a church that no method could fix, I was forced to move to the back seat and allow

Jesus to steer. I was there to love the people who were on the ride with me and to invite others to ride along. By learning to love the driver of the church—Jesus—I became passionately involved in his moves and not mine. It's this passion that will move the church forward in the 21st century.

As I look back over this time of pastoring what has been deemed an innovative, postmodern church, I see that Jesus drives the church as well as reclines in the back seat with us. Learning how to be in the back seat will allow God's power to take the front seat. What happened in Acts 2? God empowered the Church. What's still happening in the 21st century? God's still empowering the church.

Whenever I travel, I'm not just a little bothered in the back seat—sometimes I really hate it. Riding in the back seat can make me nauseated and sick! I enjoy being in control. On a recent 13-hour road trip with my family, I wouldn't let anyone else drive. Why? Because I didn't trust anyone else behind the wheel. Yet at the end of the drive, I was tired and worn out. Likewise, in pastoring, we have to let go of the wheel to ride with Jesus in the back seat. Let God be your power source, your planning resource, and your provision to move your church into this new millennium. Without God's power, the church is an institution parading around with another group of plans and activities. The world isn't looking for more activities, but a place where power and passion make sense with life.

Jesus knew how to turn a simple drink of water into living water. Ask the woman at the well in John 4. We've heard a lot in the church-growth movement about being purpose-driven. However, I contend that the purpose doesn't drive us—it's the power of God that drives us and the purpose of God that navigates the power. God's purpose is to redeem people. It was Jesus' passionate love that allowed his purpose to stop at a well. At Hillvue Heights, I've learned that without God's power, all things work out to be nothing. In God's power, even impossible moments—like the woman at the well—become possible. For example, a church that experts said couldn't possibly grow, grew not from demographic analysis, but by divine impartation. I know this church. It's the one I've been living with for almost 10 years.

THREE VIEWS FROM THE BACK SEAT

GOD'S POWER

God's power is available to every living, breathing person. God's power is available to all pastors—not some pastors. However, most of us don't realize God's power because we want to drive instead of follow. We want to be the vision instead of live the vision. To experience God's power, one needs to go to the back seat and let the Spirit of God be the navigator and purpose-driver of the church. This goes against the natural desire of a leader—to control. It means that staff meetings, board meetings, and worship planning need to be about 90 percent prayer and 10 percent planning. Pray for spiritual ears to hear the vibe of God.

What does God desire? God wants to bless people. Yet we want to be the one blessing instead of the coordinator of the blessing. I can't bless the people. I learned in an impossible situation in 1991 that people don't grow churches; the Spirit of God grows churches. I was crazy enough to believe that only God could move in a dilapidated building, $450,000 in debt, and 30 people who didn't believe the church experts when they were instructed to close the doors.

What have I learned? I've learned to make myself available to be the conduit of God's power. How available have you been to God's power? How many hours have you spent in prayer? How many moments have you asked God what he wants to do in your church? Until you dwell in the power of God, you're nothing more than an organizer. Pastors don't need to be organizers; they need to be synergizers of God's power in this world. I've learned that the power of God draws all kinds of people to him. In reality, God's in charge of his church.

GOD'S PASSION

The second view I've learned from sitting in the back seat is that we can be passionate about God's work. Hillvue Heights has learned to be passionate through worship. You don't worship to believe; you worship like you believe. When you walk into a church and there's a fervent power of God circulating with passionate worship, you have to ask yourself these questions: Is God at work here? Is this the Holy Spirit? Why are these people so consumed by the work of God? Why do they sing? Why do they express their worship so openly? Why would they praise God? Why would they welcome me? What has a hold on them? God's passion will move mountains. God wants his passion to be in all his people—it's contagious.

We've found the contagious passion of God to be in every event we practice in the life of Hillvue Heights. Passionate worship, from the singing to the welcoming to the preaching to the altar, needs to vibrate with the Spirit of God's love for his people. We've discovered at Hillvue Heights that fervent worship is an attraction to the non-Christian, not a deterrent. In fact, first-time seekers are mesmerized and uncomfortably comforted, and have brought many people back for the next Sunday's celebration. Whatever we do, we want to do it with the fervency and the urgency of God.

God's passion is that none perish. God's power and his passion are the key ingredients to experiencing a church with impact. Is your passion in creating a large church or in expressing the passionate love God has for people?

GOD'S LOVE

The third view from the back seat is God's love for his people.

The church is about being so filled with God's love that it'll bless people. The church is always about people. At Hillvue Heights, we use the slogan "A Place for All People." As the church attempts to coordinate, orchestrate, organize, and (heaven forbid) institutionalize, may we not forget that the church has always been about people. God's love will drive a grandmother to stuff her ears with cotton so her grandchildren may hear the gospel in a language they can understand. This grandmother does whatever it takes so the world might know Jesus. What are you doing to lead people in your city away from hell and toward heaven? It's about people gathering to praise. It's about people gathering to serve. It's about people gathering to pray. It's about people gathering to experience God's love and our new life together in Christ.

As I look out from the back seat, I would recommend that all of us who serve God faithfully have this perspective in our lives. We need to be overwhelmed by God's power, motivated by God's passion, and in love with God's people. Let God's power drive the church. Be so wrapped up in trusting God that you'll even let God have the steering wheel. What's God's purpose? "God... would have all to come to know Jesus Christ and come to a knowledge of the truth" (1 Timothy 2:3-4). It's that all would come to know Jesus Christ and all would dwell in heaven, so the passion of wanting to see every human being connected with God should be the passion of our hearts. At Hillvue Heights, we've never forgotten that the church is always about people. This is especially true when it comes to our buildings, our plans, and our technology. We make sure that whatever we're doing is blessing people and not just fulfilling another ministry activity.

I encourage you as you move from the driver's seat to the back seat to make sure that three standing stones are left in your ministry. Are you flowing in the power of God? Have you transmitted the passion of Jesus' love for you? Have you kept your eyes on Jesus in order to love people as he loves them? May God bless your 21st-century church as the church of Jesus Christ raises her head with power and beauty and blesses a world of chaos—a world that God so loves.

WHAT LEADERS DO

by ALAN NELSON | *(September/October 1997)*

Most leaders don't lead—most of the time.

Typically, they look for effective leaders, analyze them, and then say they're studying leadership. So maybe they focus on King David's leadership style, trying to learn what works and what doesn't. But leaders don't do leadership. They lead.

The character traits we're admonished to develop in 1 Timothy hold true for any mature believer but give us little insight into how to lead effectively. Simply put, most of the things leaders are expected to do don't involve leading.

I'm a father, but if you followed me during the course of my day, you'd see me do many things that have little or nothing to do with fatherhood. Calling those tasks "fathering" would be misleading. In the same way, leaders spend most of their time managing, teaching, counseling, doing public relations, training, and any number of other non-leading tasks.

The difference between effective leaders and mediocre leaders or non-leaders is that effective leaders recognize when the situation demands a leader. We need leaders when a team must be built, when a vision needs to be cast, when policies need to be established that affect the effectiveness (not the efficiency) of an organization, and when the big picture needs to be addressed.

Church leaders need to know how to preach, strategize, teach, and manage, but if they're to be effective in a changing world, they must know when and how to lead. When we manage, teach, or perform some other role—when we need to be leading—our congregations will suffer and our leader teams will languish.

THE SIGNIFICANCE SNARE

by SCOTT LARSEN | *(May/June 2000)*

We often feel that our significance comes from the success of our ministries. Listen to one who's traveled that road and discovered his significance isn't in what he does, but in whose he is.

"If this is all there is to being a Christian, I'm not sure it's enough for me." I remember how frightening it was when that thought first crossed my mind. I was 23 years old and had a successful career as a stockbroker. I had a great car and a house, I tithed 10 percent of my income, I volunteered as a youth worker through a local ministry, and I led a reasonably faithful life in service to God…yet I was desperately confused.

All my dreams had come true. But suddenly I wasn't sure it was enough. I was concerned about coming to the end of my life and realizing I'd only made rich people richer. I wanted my life to make a bigger difference than this. Didn't God have more for me?

That's how God calls many of us into full-time ministry. By his grace we achieve our goals, and then ask if that's all there is.

We desire to shift from the paradigm of success to one of significance. And while at first that sounds noble, it can also be extremely damaging—not only to ourselves but to those whom we've been called to serve.

FROM HOPE TO HARDSHIP

When I left my job and entered seminary at age 24, I was filled with the hope of making a significant impact in peoples' lives. Sensing God's leading to work with troubled teens, in 1987 my wife Hanne and I launched a ministry in the juvenile jails of New England. Soon after, we recognized the great need for after-care, and so we opened a discipleship home for released juvenile offenders.

The only thing tougher than that first year of living with juvenile delinquents was the second year. By its end I felt burned out, used up, spiritually dry, profoundly disappointed, and very angry. I'd left my successful career to work with a handful of troubled teens, and they didn't seem to be getting any better. In fact, it looked more like they were getting worse.

All I'd wanted was to make a difference—for my life to have lasting significance. Had I missed God's calling? And where was all this anger coming from? It got so bad that at one point I couldn't even attend our evening devotions because of the anger and hatred I was harboring toward one of the boys living with us. I couldn't stand being in the same room with him.

I began meeting with an older accountability partner, trying to understand what God was saying in all of this. In the process I came to realize that my dominant need was to make a lasting, significant difference. That's why I left a successful career as a stockbroker to go to seminary. It's why I chose to go into full-time ministry. It's why I believed that opening a home for juvenile offenders was a worthwhile sacrifice.

While that's a noble desire, I had a faulty understanding of where my ultimate sense of significance comes from. It can only be found in Jesus Christ. God graciously grants us significant and worthwhile things to do in this life, but our deepest needs for significance will never be met in those things. Only he can meet that need.

REDISCOVERING GOD'S REALITY

The lights went on for me one day when I realized that a handful of juvenile delinquents had the power to control whether I felt my life was worthwhile or not. By their actions, or lack of them, they controlled whether or not I felt significant. It was a recipe for disaster. No wonder I had so much anger and hatred toward them. I had entrusted them with a responsibility that only God could handle.

I've met many pastors and ministry leaders who feel the same sense of disappointment and anger. They too had left all to follow Christ. And somehow it didn't turn out the way they'd envisioned. They wanted to make a difference, to do something significant. But now when the parishioners, or prisoners, or homeless, or whoever they felt called to, weren't changing fast enough, a deep-seated anger toward them began to fester. And they began to question God.

In John 6:66 many followers of Jesus were beginning to feel disillusioned by some of the things he was saying. "From this time many of his disciples turned back and no longer followed him." Their expectations weren't being met. This wasn't what they'd envisioned when they joined up with this Galilean. At one point Jesus even asked the 12, "Do you want to leave too?"

I can relate to Peter's response, "Lord, to whom shall we go?" I felt like I was already in this too deep to turn back and return to what I was doing before. Like Peter, I felt caught in the middle. I didn't want to go back to what I had before, but I didn't know enough to go forward either. How could I move beyond that middle ground?

A new day dawned for me when I began laying aside my expectations for gaining significance out of ministry. I confessed to God that I had needed these kids to change so that I could feel significant, and that was wrong.

I also stopped trying to figure out how I could get out of the home we were running. Instead I began praying, "Lord, please use this home to change me. It's obvious that I'm in need of changing. I've never seen that so clearly as I do now. And I'm convinced that you've placed me here to do a deeper work in me than might otherwise have been possible. I won't leave here until you're finished or until you tell me to go."

Now I was in a position where I could embrace, rather than fight, what God wanted to do in me so that ultimately he could better work through me to reach others. And quite surprisingly, as a result I was beginning to see more instances where God was using me to make a significant difference. Only now I could see it as an unexpected act of his grace, not something I deserved because of my efforts. And what a difference that's made.

TEN REASONS FOR LEADERSHIP FAILURE

by ROBERT JOHNSON | *(November/December and January/February 2005)*

Why do leaders sometimes fail? Why do people either refuse to follow or choose to stop following? After 15 years of being involved in pastoral leadership, I've been reflecting a great deal on this critical question. Below are some of my conclusions thus far, pulled from the classroom of personal experiences. Here are my top 10 reasons why leaders sometimes fail.

1. Leaders fail when they don't communicate consistently and effectively with their followers. It's amazing how many leaders expect people to follow them when those followers are confused or uninformed about where they're going or what they're doing. At worst, the lack of communication leads to pervasive fear and frustration. When people don't know anything, they imagine everything!

2. Leaders fail when they ignore how group culture impacts leadership. Culture not only reflects the beliefs, core values, and fundamental assumptions of a community, but it controls how people communicate and how people interpret communication. For example, it's hard for a leader to earn trust while sustaining—intentionally or unintentionally—a culture of mistrust. In such a situation, any attempt to communicate trust results in compounded mistrust.

3. Leaders fail when they're inconsistent. Inconsistency creates insecurity. And grown-ups need security just as much as infants and toddlers.

4. Leaders fail when their lives are inconsistent with the vision they espouse. I've seen people follow leaders, even when the leaders make mistakes. Why? Because the followers know that the leader burns with real passion and commitment for the vision. However, people won't follow leaders who point in one direction for the followers but commit themselves to another.

5. Leaders fail when they don't champion the needs of the people they lead. Successful leaders advocate visions that are deeply rooted in the needs, dreams, and aspirations of the followers. People generally don't care about things that don't impact either their present or their future. When a vision doesn't really matter to people, they may not oppose it, but they'll certainly not labor sacrificially for it either.

6. Leaders fail when they don't have the courage to champion their visions. A leader can have others do a lot of things to help bring a vision into reality, but ultimately the vision has to have a champion, and that's the role of the leader. Unfortunately, many leaders allow their need to be liked to diminish their passion for the vision.

7. Leaders fail when they lack the personal fortitude and resiliency necessary to see a vision through in spite of opposition and setbacks. No vision comes to be without struggles, disappointments, setbacks, rejections, and loss, and the greater the vision the greater will be the challenges to making it reality. At the critical moments, even when everyone else is ready to "throw in the towel," the leader's role is to "dig deep" and rally the team forward.

8. Leaders fail when they allow the "snakes" to survive and thrive. Snakes are the people in your organization who harbor ill will for the organization or who have demonstrated an aggressive discontent for the organization. Christian leaders certainly should seek ways to "redeem" people for the sake of the kingdom, but there are times when a person's redemption will not happen within the realm of your church. When such a person overtly or covertly undermines the mission, he or she needs to be released and disconnected from the organization.

9. Leaders fail when they reject the presence and gifts of the radicals. I'm not impressed with people who are radical for the sake of being radical. On the other hand, I think that it's difficult to keep an organization fresh and vital unless the leader from time to time injects the culture and processes with a healthy dose of "what has never been done before!" You don't have to embrace the radicals' perspectives, but at least hear them out. And every now and then, take a radical leap. At the least, don't run the radicals away!

10. Leaders fail when they underestimate the adversary. Over and over, leaders make the mistake of thinking that they are untouchable, immune, or exempt from failure, which in turn leads to failure. A wise leader rejoices in every victory but faces the next challenge as if it's the first one.

HEY, COACH
*The Benefits of Partnering
With a Leadership Coach*

by ALAN NELSON | *(January/February 2003)*

Growing up on an Iowa farm, I remember how easy it was to get your vehicle stuck after a heavy rain, snow, or spring thaw. Sometimes rocking the car back and forth allowed you to drive out of a potential trap. But at other times, spinning your tires only bogged you down until all hope was gone. Ministry in the 21st century is a muddy venture. Getting stuck is becoming easier—what's a pastor to do?

When I got stuck in Iowa, occasionally a more knowledgeable person came along and coached me, giving me advice such as: "Don't spin your tires, you'll go deeper," or "If you back up, there's gravel that will give you traction." At other times, an ally would bounce my car's bumper or nudge it with his vehicle, something I couldn't do for myself while behind the wheel.

A growing trend among marketplace organizations is executive coaching. The strategy of coaching is to help the leader get unstuck. While executive coaching can focus on multiple areas of improvement, what's needed most often in church work is leadership coaching—coaching that helps pastors enhance their leading skills. Those unfamiliar with this professional practice might think of coaching as a remedial process, but top corporate leaders are now seeking help as never before. Even Tiger Woods has been traveling with a swing coach for 10 years.

If the world's #1 golf entertainer uses coaches to keep improving his game, all of us would do well to consider the potential of coaching in our field, where the risks have eternal impact. The pursuit of coaching comes from a desire to do your best and not being too proud to ask someone for insight.

WHY DO WE NEED A COACH?

One might think that with the plethora of leadership resources available, these would be sufficient to create more and better leaders. If literature were enough to unstick leaders, we'd be in great shape, with so many volumes shouting instructions to us. Personally, I have more than 400 leadership books in my collection, but no book I've seen contains the silver bullet for leadership. The primary reason is that books and conferences tend to be impersonal and one-way in communication.

However, when a coach comes into the picture, that person helps the leader translate the salient points in a book, conference, or consultation into the language of his or her specific context and skills. To twist an ancient adage: Give a man a leadership book or conference and he'll lead for a day; teach (coach) him to lead and he'll lead for a lifetime.

When a pastor feels stuck, he has the tendency to either look for greener grass or give up on the inside, assuming things aren't going to get better—due to the church or personal limitations. The typical pastoral tenure is an average of three to four years, yet longevity in the ministry is one of the proven elements of ministerial fruitfulness. However, sticking around because you're stuck won't magically make your ministry effective and your congregation productive.

Speaking at the Prayer Quake in Mesa, Arizona, Bill McCartney said that a study revealed that nine out of 10 pastors feel discouraged. We want to make progress, but it seems as though we're just spinning our wheels. Conrad Lowe says this may be one reason why up to 50 percent of pastors leave the ministry within the first 10 years of their careers. Staying in one church, but not being stuck in one place, is important—and we all need help from time to time to give us a nudge in the right direction. A good coach can do that. Finding the right help is sometimes all it takes to turn an overwhelming and frustrating situation into a pivotal point of growth and fulfillment.

A leadership coach is someone who walks with you for a season, steps into your life as a pastor/minister, and provides feedback, a different perspective. And when appropriate, a nudge to move you forward. This person is trained to speak into your life as few others can. Typically, leaders are surrounded by people who love them without telling them the truth and by those who tell them the truth without loving them. Most of us lack people in our lives who have the confidence to speak with both grace and informed honesty. After you get a haircut, the stylist hands you a mirror and turns your chair so you can see the back of your head. A significant goal of a leadership coach is to hold up a mirror to show you what you may not be able to see on your own.

THE FOUNDATION FOR COACHING

While the marketplace trend of executive coaching is likely to become a growing practice in the complex field of the 21st-century church, ministry leadership coaching actually dates back to Jethro advising Moses on how to do things differently in order to be more effective (Exodus 18). Leadership is the focal point for strategic improvement, so leaders are the key in any organizational changes. According to George Barna and others, if our churches are to become life-transformation centers of the 21st century, we must unleash leaders who will do what's necessary to catalyze leadership. Books are great and conferences are better, but the missing link is hands-on and personalized development methods.

Ironically, we as Christians often pride ourselves on our humility, yet we're unwilling to admit our need for help in developing our leadership potential, and our churches suffer as a result. The eternal destination of people around us demands that we become more aggressive in the way we conduct our work.

COACHING QUESTIONS

Question: How is coaching different than counseling, consulting, mentoring, and training?

Answer: Since coaching is relatively new to most leaders, let's compare it with more familiar development processes. Coaching often takes the form of methods such as counseling, consulting, mentoring, and training, but generally differs from these methods.

Coaching vs. Counseling: Coaching tends to focus on the here-and-now and the future, while counseling often delves into past influences. Coaching tends to deal more in professional issues and public actions; counseling on personal and private.

Coaching vs. Consulting: Coaching tends to focus on leader development, whereas consulting targets organizational matters. Coaching helps the leader unleash his or her potential so that the organization receives the benefits.

Coaching vs. Mentoring: Coaching tends to focus on specific goals, whereas mentoring is often more generic. Coaching is done by a person who's trained in coaching, whereas a mentor is often one who has experience but has little expertise in transferring strategic knowledge.

Coaching vs. Training: Coaching tends to coax the answers out of the leader, while training is about telling him or her what to do or think. It relies more on asking the right questions than on providing set solutions to problems, thus improving process skills more than merely outcome specifics.

Question: Why is there a trend toward leadership coaching?

Answer: There are three main reasons for this cultural movement.

1. The world in which we live is more complex than ever, requiring a constant need to learn and improve. Multiple organizational demands distract leaders from making proactive, reflective investigations of their potential.

No one has a corner on the market of what it takes to succeed. The complexity of leading today requires that we dig deeper into our potential and develop it. The sheer number of situations demanding leading means that those inadequately prepared and only modestly gifted are like fish out of water, trying to respond outside of their comfort zones. Improving often requires the help of trained specialists, much like a professional athlete incorporates coaches, trainers, and managers to maximize his or her potential.

2. We've discovered that no cookbook or canned programs exist that will "fix" us or our churches. Coaching helps us find our answers in our specific ministry contexts by focusing on us as church influencers. Personalized assessments and feedback transcend books and conferences and allow for more personal interaction. While books, conferences, and resources are abundant, there's often a disconnect between the event and the ministry context. Therefore a coach assists the leader in bridging the gap between concept and action, significant ideas and implementation. The reason Jesus invested primarily in a few versus investing in the masses was more than likely because he understood that the power of enduring transformation must be individualized rather than broadcast, assisted rather than self-learned. You can't mass-produce leaders, no matter how good the author, scholar, or trainer.

3. Larger churches, parachurch ministries, and denominational organizations—like their marketplace

counterparts—are realizing that finding competent leaders is often difficult. The competition for naturally great leaders squeezes most organizations out of the market. Plus, leader and staff transitions create organizational turmoil and often disrupt effectiveness. Coaching pays off emotionally and financially by investing in an existing team member versus trying to find someone from the outside. Promoting a person to his or her own level of incompetence (the Peter Principle) can often be avoided with adequate coaching and development.

Question: When's the best time to have a coach?

Answer: Bringing in a coach to improve a leader's effectiveness usually has a more positive feel than a crisis consultant or even a personal counselor does—largely because of the common use of coaches in business, professional sports, and the arts. The idea of unleashing latent potential has a proactive feel, instead of fixing the problem of someone who's doing a lousy job. Here are five common situations when leadership coaching and concentrated leadership development make sense in a church or typical organization:

Leadership coaching makes the most sense when a leader feels stuck, has been in a ministry for three years or more with little or no growth, or deeply desires to hone skills that can enhance his or her leading abilities.

Leadership coaching takes on a more proactive role when an organization has experienced significant growth

and the leader is motivated to keep pace and perpetu-
ate momentum by developing more of his or her leader
potential.

A board or leader may bring in a coach to invest in the
life of a promising staff member, in hopes that the person
can ramp up to the next level and not have to be replaced.
Here it's important that the recipient has motivation,
which will make the coaching effective. A new staffer
who is coached has a better chance of getting acclimated
more quickly and is apt to stay longer.

Leadership coaching takes on special effectiveness
when a significant change process is underway. While a
change consultant may be important as well, one primary
element of any transition formula is that it's leader-
oriented. Thus, a coach can become a key factor in guid-
ing a leader through a change process.

Leadership coaching can also take the form of staff
training when creating a leadership culture within a
church—thus enhancing the leader's ability to lead. A
jump-start—such as a staff retreat—is a means of ramp-
ing up the leadership of a group in addition to an individual.

Question: How does a coaching process work?

Answer: A leader determines the need to get unstuck or
unleash untapped potential. A board may do this for its
leader, or a pastor may do this for a staff member or even
a team of staff. Part of this consideration is to be honest
about your coachability. Some suggest that only about
20 percent of people are coachable, mostly because the

other 80 percent are either too proud to seek help or they are unwilling to act on the emergent insights. This is key to the entire process, because a leader who lacks motivation to change usually won't.

Contact is made with a leadership coach. This is the time where introductions take place, goals and expectations are established, confidentiality is confirmed, and estimated costs and timelines are discussed. A written contract is often prepared and signed for clarity.

Initial in-depth assessments are completed. The specific assessment tends to be determined by the goals. This more than likely involves a face-to-face meeting, often in the leader's work context. Surveys, personality or leadership skill composites, and 360-degree feedback may be gathered.

Subsequent meetings focus on issues that arise from the feedback, goals that are set, and problems that emerge. This free flow may involve elements of action items, training, accountability, and further measuring. Often these discussions take place on the phone and via e-mail, making cost and scheduling reasonable.

Follow-up may be negotiated in the agreement. If agreed upon, a coach is available as needed for feedback and debriefing after the concentrated coaching period.

Question: What do I look for in a coach?

Answer: Right now, there are very few church leadership coaches. This author is developing a network of such people, but here are some things to look for when seeking leadership coaching in a ministry context.

You're going to want to find someone you enjoy and with whom you have a sense of affinity and trust. In addition, look for a coach who's familiar with your ministry context but more importantly, is an expert in leadership development. Because the coaching field is still young, there are no required credentials for being a coach. Being certified as a coach is a start, but obviously isn't a guarantee of effectiveness. You'll want to make sure the coach is savvy in the areas where you desire help.

Realize that star practitioners rarely make the best coaches. You'll probably never see Michael Jordan, Barry Bonds, or Wayne Gretzky as coaches. Phil Jackson was a modest NBA player but is a top-notch coach. While exceptional talents frequently get quoted and become teachers, they rarely have the time for coaching, and quite often, they're not aware of what it is that makes them so effective. The skill set required to be insightful as a coach often eludes the superstars.

Find someone who has an ability to facilitate processes over merely teaching (dumping) new ideas. People who push a specific program or who train tend to give too many answers and thus fail to assist the leader in growing by under-utilizing questions, feedback retrieval, and intuitive dialogue.

Most leadership coaches have gifts of leadership mixed with gifts of discernment, knowledge, and spiritual sensitivity. Because our goal isn't just better leading but more effective spiritual leading, combining the two is vital. The question of godly wisdom and leadership expertise is not "either-or" but "both-and."

The Peter Principle says that people tend to rise to the level of their incompetence. Leadership coaching advocates a Simon Peter Principle. Jesus called Simon, *petros*, meaning "rock." At the time, Simon was everything but rock solid, an emotionally driven reactionary. But he eventually lived up to his new name because of the divine coaching he received. In other words, he moved beyond his natural level of incompetence, realizing his greater potential. If we fail to develop our leaders, we shouldn't be surprised with the mediocre level of leading. The word *mediocre* literally means "halfway up the mountain." Leadership coaching is a 21st-century means of maximizing a leader's potential by helping him or her climb further up the hill.

THE POTENTIAL BENEFITS OF COACHING

The power of an outside voice often frees us from internal blinders common in local church work

A biblical premise behind coaching is relying on the gifts of discernment and knowledge from someone who's trained to bring out the best in you, thus building up the body of Christ. Assuming you can reach deep down into your potential and mine your gold yourself is often naive, if not prideful.

Familiarity breeds blind spots, so we sabotage our effectiveness.

No one would question our motives, commitment, or zeal, but perspective is critical. A little tweaking by Jethro revolutionized the way Moses led. No one could deny the anointing, the willingness to sacrifice, or the call of God in Moses' life, but he was still stuck, on the verge of burnout. To keep doing what we've done and yet hope for different results is nothing short of neurotic. Jesus often utilized a coaching style with his disciples, asking them key questions that created new ways of thinking and responding to situations. The result was developed leaders.

Working with a coach for leader and staff development is often good stewardship when conferences and travel costs can become prohibitive. Add to that the breakdown in translating conference principles into the unique context of your ministry situation, and the net yield can be low. When you begin with your ministry idiosyncrasies, you increase the likelihood of gaining productive insights. The more individualistic and personal approach of coaching allows a firsthand view of the leader within his or her ministry context.

The goal of leadership coaching is a more confident and competent leader, increasing the value of the leader to the organization. Investing in team members adds effectiveness to the organization. Investing in leaders multiplies it. Strategically investing five to 10 percent of a leader's salary into growth and self-improvement can yield far greater results than the same money spent on a raise, a new computer, or office furniture. This enhances the chances for leader longevity, not to mention fulfillment.

THE QUEST FOR LEADERSHIP DEVELOPMENT

by JEFF STRONG | *(September/October 2004)*

Aristotle once noted, "Those who wish to succeed must ask the right preliminary questions." When it comes to success in the area of leadership development, I couldn't agree more.

Leadership development is, foundationally, the process of asking the right people the right questions. To that end, I believe there are five questions every leader needs to be asking throughout the leadership development process. Whether the context is their family, their leadership team, their mentoring relationship, or within their peer group, there are five foundational questions that, when coupled with trust and genuine engagement, result in transformational leadership development.

These are the questions that give us the right as leaders to speak into the hearts and lives of those we lead, and these are questions that continually pull us back to "first things"—in both our professional and personal lives.

I've come to appreciate and recognize that while those in leadership recognize the high value of leadership development conceptually, exactly how to go about facilitating it is anything but intuitive. For example, despite the gluttonous supply of resources that exist on the subject of mentoring and coaching leaders, attempts to use these resources often result in more confusion and complexity. Somewhere between our good intentions and our leadership development goals, understanding and common sense gets replaced with programmed interactions and detached communication theory, and what should be natural and relational becomes mechanical.

The questions offered are neither revolutionary nor transformative in and of themselves. They're not magical or novel. They are, however, questions that, when coupled with an intent to understand and appreciate the other, will initiate and support an ongoing interaction—one whose fruit will be transformative in nature.

QUESTION 1: WHO ARE YOU?

Rev. Thoughts: Be intentional during this time of your leadership development. If you begin your leadership development through relational means, you'll see the same thing replicated in the ministries that are birthed out of this group of leadership. Remember—leadership leaks. Always ask yourself, *"What am I leaking to my leaders that will be leaked to our congregation?"*

This question, while seemingly simplistic, is anything but simple or redundant. You can't lead clearly if you don't know who you are. And you can't lead clearly if you don't know the people you're leading. Knowing who you're leading is foundational to all of your subsequent leadership development efforts as well. No programs, practices, or procedures will compensate for ignoring or bypassing this critical question. So often leaders are more concerned with the information they're sharing than the transformation that can occur when you lead in relationship.

Invite members of your leadership team to share their stories and spiritual journeys. Move beyond the assumptions or preconceived notions you have concerning who they are and what they're about. Listen with your ears and your heart as you attempt to discern the patterns of experiences God's weaving into the leaders before you. Take the time to explore this question and help them articulate how God has been orchestrating their spiritual formation. During this time of intentional relationship building, you'll build stronger bridges of trust, foster a relational climate, and allow for openness and authenticity to become a core value.

QUESTION 2: WHAT ARE YOU LEARNING?

As a leader you're keenly aware that the pace at which your circle of knowledge grows is matched only by the growth of its outer edge of ignorance. Remember that as you go about developing the leaders in your midst. As a trusted leader you can become an invaluable source of support and encouragement as

Rev. Thoughts: One of the greatest opportunities the church is missing is in the area of archiving, reflecting, and debriefing. We're so busy with the "what's next" in our ministry that we forget to learn from our past experiences. Make this looking back a priority throughout your church's ministries and operations.

you compel them to internalize and process their experiences. Ask them what they're learning as they go about their day-to-day responsibilities. If you can help them hone this skill, it will become one of your greatest gifts to them. Teach them to create a format that allows them to archive their experiences. Whether it's journaling, debriefing, or keeping files, consistently encourage them to ask themselves the question, What are you learning? Intentionally ask them to comment and reflect on their experiences in the areas they've been entrusted with in their ministry. Don't hesitate to suggest that they occasionally write some kind of ministry reflection paper, or a comparable activity that forces them to digest and express the lessons they're learning.

QUESTION 3: WHERE ARE YOU STRUGGLING?

Rarely is everyone you're leading doing fine. In fact, assume that there are those in your group who are dealing with issues in their lives. In many cases, people feel overwhelmed and humbled by what they're

Rev. Thoughts: This is a sensitive area in leadership. Many leaders feel their ministry could be in question if they were to reveal any signs of weakness. Encourage your team by being authentic with them regarding your life and ministry. Understand the boundaries of transparency, but also be willing to share with them some of your own struggles, questions, and victories both personally and professionally. And remember the C word—*confidentiality.*

facing both personally and professionally as they attempt to bring their sense of vocation into clarity. It goes without saying that there are some areas of their lives that they'll be unwilling to open up to you about until sufficient trust has been established, but don't assume that means they're not willing to open up at all. Likewise, there are people who aren't prone to sharing things with others, so don't place any unnecessary pressure on them. In a culture of high trust, people are usually aware of their blind spots, generally willing to admit their shortcomings, and are encouraged when they're gently pushed out of the self-reliant, individualistic paradigm of our culture. This aspect of leadership development, however, can only be achieved by open discussions surrounding the struggles and victories of the team.

QUESTION 4: WHAT DO YOU THINK?

The emerging leaders around you have something to contribute. But some leadership teams don't have an atmosphere where team members feel like they can speak up. If they do speak up, they often refrain from presenting their real idea, only to present a creatively

Rev. Thoughts: Be creative. Create a room or tools that open the door for thinking out loud or brainstorming. Whether it's a set of cards or some fun object, set the ground rules that no idea is a bad idea. Teach your leadership teams how to brainstorm ideas and what process should follow. Find resources that will allow for this function to grow within your leadership development program.

sanitized version. Two warnings: First, don't be guilty of creating an atmosphere where people think you're only interested in your own ideas. Second, push back on your leaders by asking them their opinions on everything—from lighting in the church to current leadership issues. Develop an atmosphere of creative thinking and solutions. Listen to them and consider their perspectives seriously. It goes without saying that you can take their ideas or leave them, but providing space where they can be honest and open with their opinions will result in an uncommon creative synergy between team members, and everyone's ministry will be stronger as a result.

QUESTION 5: HOW CAN I HELP?

This is perhaps the sweetest-sounding question of all to someone who at times feels like they're floundering in ministry—which is all of us. People who are involved in any kind of leadership development process are doing their best. But their best will be improved

Rev. Thoughts: You should become a "resource broker" for your leaders. Be about the business of identifying the latest and greatest books to read, identifying churches and their leaders who have already done what you've done, discovering curriculum and resources that will further your mission, and creating space in your own ministry to pour into the lives of your leaders. Your resourcing will leak into their lives and will leak through them into the lives of those people they're leading.

if you're willing to give them input, suggestions, or be a sounding board whenever possible. Again, you're modeling to them what it means to be a leader, and they'll in turn do the same thing with the leaders they're developing. Having someone in your corner who understands your needs and does what they can to support you is communicating the very essence of servant leadership. Leadership today is collaboration more than autonomy. Most leaders don't want to go it alone. Sometimes your leaders will be able to look you in the eye and honestly say, "I'm OK, thanks." But more often, especially in the beginning of leadership training, your "How can I help?" will be a lifeline for them as they navigate the waters of ministry.

PRE-QUESTION: WHERE DO I START?

Leadership development, like any leadership endeavor, requires an inside-out approach. Therefore, the first step begins by engaging these five questions personally. Whether through journaling, coaching, or dialoguing with a trusted friend, explore these questions within your own life. Take time to hear God and what he's speaking to you through these questions. Remember: You can't lead those you don't know—and that includes yourself.

If you want to develop the leaders around you, keep relationship as a core value in your leadership development program. Remember that Jesus surrounded himself with 12 men…and the rest is history.

AND YOU CALL YOURSELF A LEADER

By ALAN NELSON | *(September/October 2005)*

I don't like the word *obsessive* because…well, it reminds me of myself. Fifteen years ago, I began my formal quest to discover what it was that made leaders different than others. I'd always been curious about leadership, but had never studied it deeply. I started a doctorate in the field at the University of San Diego, attended more than one $4,000 Center for Creative Leadership program and too-many-to-mention seminars and conferences, interviewed numerous leaders, and collected 600-plus leadership books. This has been in addition to actually trying to lead for more than 20 years in local congregations.

TRADITIONAL CHURCH PARADIGM	THE COMING WORK-LIFE CHURCH
• The organization of the church is the mission.	• The daily lives of those in the church is the mission.
• Sermons speak in "churchese" about church categories and topics.	• Sermons talk in marketplace-friendly language about being salt and light at work.
• Bible stories are told through a ministry lens.	• Bible characters are painted in all their humanity and daily living.
• Illustrations are primarily from the pastor's personal world.	• Illustrations are from the work-a-day world of the audience.
• Members are pressured to make church a priority over work.	• Church structure is simplified to free leaders to fulfill their callings.
• Church health is measured in attendance and buildings.	• Health is measured by the impact of the church's footprint in the community.
• Everyone is expected to come to the physical location of the church for ministry.	• The church initiates training, relationships, and programs out into the marketplace.
• Spiritual formation is focused on church assimilation.	• Spiritual formation includes work-life issues of calling, serving, skill, and character development.
• Training and mobilization focus on staffing and maintaining the church program.	• Training and mobilization includes facilitating spiritual entrepreneurship.

An expert is someone who knows a lot about very little. Don't get me wrong. I didn't say I was a great leader. I'm just more familiar with what others say about the subject than is probably healthy. *Leadership* has been a "buzz" word the last 20 years, primarily because, as if you haven't heard, society has been undergoing tumultuous changes. A leader is only necessary when change is required. If everything's going well, enlist a good manager but avoid a leader at all costs, because he or she will try to disrupt the status quo.

If you're like me, you're bored with vanilla articles on leadership, such as "Seven Easy Steps to Becoming a Better Leader!" So for your edification and maybe to avoid a yawn myself, let me share five potentially disturbing summaries regarding contemporary leadership and everyday church life from my perspective as a leadership analyst and pastor.

1. LEADERSHIP IS OVERRATED AND UNDERUTILIZED

Unlike some might suggest, everything doesn't rise and fall on leadership. The leadership gurus would like to make you think that, especially if they have a book or conference on the subject to sell. This is an example of reductionism—presenting complexities as if they're simple. Life is complicated. Suggesting that leadership alone is sufficient to fix our churches and cure our social woes lacks responsibility. Leadership is important, but it's not the silver bullet that many would want you to believe. Leadership is a very important part of solving organizational and social issues, but it's not the only one.

While better leadership isn't the end-all solution, we can't say that we've come close to overutilizing it. Like the philosopher suggested, a lot more is said than done. I've found that reading about leading is far easier than doing the thing. By talking about leadership, we often delude ourselves into thinking we're actually practicing it. Leading effectively is far more difficult than a lot of us would like to admit. One reason for our lack of application is that most pastors and other church leaders are besieged with responsibilities in addition to leading. Everything a leader does isn't leadership. Most of the time we're preachers, counselors, nonprofit administrators, parents, spouses, evangelists, disciplers, fund-raisers, and children of God. Learning to discern when a situation needs leading, besides knowing what to do as a leader, is often a complex matter. Most of us would much rather do easier matters, whether it's sermon prep, ministry management, or pastoral care. Far too often we oil squeaking wheels when we should be leading.

2. MOST PASTORS ARE MINISTRY MANAGERS, NOT LEADERS: BUMMER OR SO WHAT?

An even bigger reason that leadership is underutilized in ministry is that most pastors really are managers instead of leaders. Ask most pastors what they enjoy about their work, and they'll likely tell you preaching, counseling, caring, evangelizing, discipling, and facilitating worship experiences for people. Most of us wear these "hats" as pastors throughout the course of a week. That's why most of us signed up for the job in the beginning. But now, something else is needed instead of management: leadership. The teaching-nurturing gift mix is most common among pastors. My informal estimate is that only 10 percent of people in the general population display organizational leadership qualities. This agrees with George Barna's findings among pastors. There's nothing wrong with this ratio, so long as we understand how we're individually wired. Paul touched on this several times in his letters. Check out these two, for example:

"It was he who gave some to be apostles, some to be prophets, some to be evangelists, and some to be pastors and teachers, to prepare God's people for works of service, so that the body of Christ may be built up until we all reach unity in the faith and in the knowledge of the Son of God and become mature, attaining to the whole measure of the fullness of Christ" (Ephesians 4:11-13).

"We have gifts that differ according to the grace given us: prophecy, in proportion to faith; ministry, in ministering; the teacher, in teaching; the exhorter, in exhortation; the giver, in generosity; the leader, in diligence; the compassionate, in cheerfulness" (Romans 12:6-8, New Revised Standard Version).

I have a great respect for the team at Leadership Journal. They turn out a great resource. Even though the title says "leadership," most of the articles in LJ are not about leading—they're about ministry. My point is not to critique the journal but to illustrate the common misconception in church work that whoever occupies the pastor's study is a leader. Positional leadership, based on title or role, is for the most part dead. It is a 20th-century, Industrial Age construct. Being called a leader no more makes you a leader than…I'm going to say it…going to McDonald's makes you a Big Mac.

Consider it a blessing to be wired the way God has designed you, regardless of your gifting. Unfortunately, we beat ourselves up trying to be like someone we're not. If you're endowed to preach, preach toward your capacity and to your heart's content. Find a place where your gift of communicating God's Word can be best utilized and serve your Creator in that role.

The problem with hyping leadership is that it gives most of us the feeling that if we're not good at leading, we're ministerial failures. Again, some guidance from Paul:

"If the foot should say, 'Because I am not a hand, I do not belong to the body,' it would not for that reason cease to be part of the body. And if the ear should say, 'Because I am not an eye, I do not belong to the body,' it would not for that reason cease to be part of the body" (1 Corinthians 12:15-16).

The problem of most pastors not being leaders is exacerbated by the next observation.

3. YOU CAN TEACH LEADERS ABOUT LEADERSHIP— BUT YOU CAN'T TURN THEM INTO LEADERS

For some unfortunate reason, church culture has bought into the American myth that you can become whatever you want. People who suggest that everyone has a leader in them, waiting to be released, perform a disservice. We end up feeling inadequate, because no matter how hard we try most of us will never be good at it. When gurus suggest that everyone can be a leader, they're usually referring to self-discipline, character, and confidence. It's a semantic game that diminishes what leadership is really about: organizing groups of people to work toward a common goal. The idea that everyone can be a leader is toxic psychologically as well as theologically.

Perhaps the problem is that those who are good at something are under the impression that everyone can be just like them.

Why is it that people who are naturally (or supernaturally) endowed with an ability, tend to be the ones who write the books and get the speaking gigs? We assume that they know why they do what they do and by explaining it, we can become like them. Is leading purely a learned skill or is it an ability that emerges from an aptitude? I've not seen a single stitch of quality research indicating that everyone has the capacity to lead.

The most gifted leaders preach to the rest about becoming leaders. The most gifted intercessors try to convince the rest of us to be more like them: prayer "warriors." Gifted evangelists make you feel guilty if you've not led your fellow airplane pals to the Lord before landing on the tarmac. If you think about it, a requirement for teaching nongifted people should be that the teacher has proven to be gifted, because gifted people do specific things naturally better than the rest of us.

Good psychology and proper theology do not support the idea that we can be whatever we desire. Life has limitations. God has graced most of us with a relatively small number of gifts. Why do we think that leading is not one of those God-given abilities?

Having said all of the above, I'm a strong advocate of teaching the process of leadership to all people so that they can understand the various functions within leadership and how the process works. Part of the reason leading is so difficult is that we've done an abysmal job of teaching nonleaders about the importance of their roles and how they fit in the whole process. Effective following is not passive as many believe. We grossly underestimate it in terms of value, power, and leader accountability. If we fail to effectively teach leadership participation as nonleaders, why do we think we can succeed as leaders?

Nonleader pastors must comprehend how leadership functions as well as how to catalyze the process from the back seat. Insecure pastors try to control staff and lay people, and as a result thwart leadership in their congregation. The alternative is when nonleader pastors pretend they know how to lead and then wonder why no one follows them. Like the fable of the emperor's clothes, few tell the pastor he or she is not a leader, but they show it by not following with diligence.

4. 21ST-CENTURY LEADERSHIP IS SIGNIFICANTLY DIFFERENT THAN ITS 20TH-CENTURY PREDECESSOR

Dinosaurs continue to roam in our midst—people who embrace a leadership style that's quickly becoming extinct. The goals of leading have pretty much remained the same throughout history. Leadership is a social process whereby groups of people work together toward common goals. As longtime management expert

Peter Drucker has stated, the primary reason of an organization is to harness our strengths and render our weaknesses useless. Because of the proliferation of education, technology for info sharing, the growth of women in the workforce, the complexity of organizations as well as the democratization of the world, old-school leading will not cut it in the 21st century.

The icon of 21st-century leading is not General George Patton, Winston Churchill, or Jack Welch as much as the Star Wars character Obi-Wan Kenobi. Leaders must take a far more humble, spiritually driven approach to leading. In my book *Spirituality & Leadership* I look at the unique challenges of being both spiritual as well as a strong leader, because leading is often toxic to your soul. Relying on human skills of manipulation, control, communication, and strategic planning are easier than delving into the spiritual realm where God and the Holy Spirit endow our gifts of influence. The CEO, top-down, linear, Great Man Theory era is quickly passing. Postmodern leading must tap the resources of the body, mind, and spirit. Even secular literature is recognizing the soul of the corporation and the need for "kinder and gentler" leading styles. Jesus' leadership style has never been more in vogue for all realms of organizational leadership.

5. THE BEST CHANCE TO CHANGE SOCIETY IS NOT THROUGH ADULT LEADERS

On my 46th birthday, I bought Bob Buford's book *Finishing Well.* I was feeling the need for a change after more than 20 years of local church work. Two church plants had nearly eaten my lunch. I was, as Bob said, starting Life 2. What bugged me about Bob's book (love ya, Bob) was that so many of the people he interviewed were guys like him. They'd been successful and made a mint during Life 1, so that they searched for significance during Life 2. I'm thinking, "What do you do if you've never had Life 1 success? Can you go for significance without being financially stable or bored out of your gourd?" Like someone said, "How can I be over the hill, if I was never on top?"

Before resigning from the seeker congregation we founded, in order to minister within the emerging spiritual movement and my Life 2 blueprint, I called 10 knowledgeable friends and asked them about their thoughts of the future in leadership development.

One friend, a guru in demographic research and cultural analysis, planted a bomb with a time-delayed fuse. He said, "Focus on the kids." Kids? Who do you think I am? I'm a professional. I have a doctorate in the field. Why would I want to focus on kids? But after a while, the bomb detonated. I got it. Let's say you have a 100-point leader scale. With training, education, and coaching you can turn a 55-point adult leader into a 60 or 65. But you can take a 40-point child leader and with age-appropriate training and mentoring, you can turn him or her into an 80-pointer.

The future of our church really is in developing kids, but not just any kids—the 10 percent who are gifted influencers who'll lead the rest. Get to the leaders when they're teachable, pliable, or, as psychologists say, possess plasticity. Character is pretty much established by age 12. Adults don't change that much. The "return on investment" is significantly lower for post-adolescents. I'm now in the research and development phase of a first-of-its-kind national program to detect and develop "tween" influencers, those in the 8 to 12 age range, where character is not yet settled and cognitions are newly elevated.

So what do we do with these five church leadership summaries, especially if we're not wired to lead? Do we boycott our annual pilgrimages to leadership summits and forego reading John Maxwell's or Tom Peters' new books? No way! We need gifted leaders to give us their perspectives on our churches. We should bring leadership teams to these events and read organizational books together. We benefit from pondering these thoughts as a group, because leadership is a social process, not just what leaders "do." At the same time, we should have realistic expectations of these conferences, books, seminars, and training events.

First of all, we need to make sure that the right people attend. Sending nonleaders to leader development events rarely turns out leaders. Pastors need to participate in the leadership process by getting staff and lay people with leadership gifts to attend conferences in order to catch vision as a team. See if the attendee has the capacity to lead, latent or other, and if not, establish realistic outcomes. Nonleader pastors must learn to drive from the back seat, unleashing gifted influencers who've been discipled to steer the vision of the church. A society with more than 10 percent leaders would likely fringe on chaotic. During times of change, we need to utilize our leaders more effectively so that their influence is multiplied by freeing them up to do what we need them to do…lead. (Read Exodus 18 again.)

Second, hold attendees, readers, and participants more accountable for their developmental investment. Intentionally leverage them. Specifically hold each other accountable. Hire a coach for at least a couple of follow-up sessions, empowering someone to ask questions such as, "What did you gain from your developmental experience?" "What do you plan to do with this information?" "How can you apply it immediately within your ministry/leadership context?" "What have you done in the first two weeks to apply this new principle?" "If you haven't implemented a change in your behavior, why haven't you?" This seldom-used practice is the equivalent of pushing the Enter key on your computer keyboard after investing numerous minutes or hours of filling the screen with meaningful data.

Third, implement a variety of learning methods if and only if you really want to "get it." Way too much effort is invested in "book learnin'" and lecture-style content dumps. Conferences are notorious for this, making us think we're gleaning far more than we really are. Hebrews 5 says that we become mature, meat-eating believers as a result of "practicing" the milk. Back to the beginning, "easier said than done." Interactive dialogue, case study analysis, experiential learning with follow-up post-mortems, and media components all serve to create a multi-sensory learning event which significantly increases the likelihood of long-term impact.

For example, look at the way that Jesus did discipleship as opposed to the typical American church. Jesus utilized a number of learning methods that transcend ours. The North American church has predominately bought into the classroom method of learning, adding a little music to worship service sermons and Sunday school Bible studies, in which basically teachers are telling us what to think. Jesus focused on four primary pedagogical methods: Teaching, Accountability, Mentoring, and Experiencing (TAME).

The perceived leadership dilemma we're supposedly in today is not going to go away soon or easily. Leaders are needed during times of change because they're the chief catalysts. We must assertively teach all participants how the leadership process works, as well as raising up a whole new generation of leaders who learn character and competencies when they are moldable. As an obsessive leadership analyst, I'm convinced that our greatest model for life and 21st-century leading is Jesus.

THE POWER OF LEARNING

by MIKE FOSS | *(November/December 2002)*

"I don't know that I agree with you," he said. "I think I've learned more from my successes than my failures."

We were a group of pastors in southern Ohio. We'd taken the time to stop the discussion we were having in order to "mine our learning." That was when the question of how we learn surfaced. I'd suggested that failures are the points at which we have the greatest possible learning. My colleague disagreed. And as I silently listened, the rest of the group entered the debate—questioning whether we learn more from our failures or our successes.

It suddenly dawned on me: We can't learn from either success or failure if we don't reflect upon it. The events teach us nothing in and of themselves. Our ability to grow our ministries through either failures or successes is dependent upon our willingness to enter a reflection process. These were the questions that have surfaced within my mind over the weeks since that significant conversation with my colleagues:

What would such a process look like?

What would be the necessary steps?

Could we enter a discipline of implementing such a process within our ministries on an ongoing basis?

THE LEARNING PROCESS

I believe the process should include at least four steps. If we follow this process, then hopefully we'll be able to learn from both our failures and successes, and apply that learning to the next events and situations we encounter in ministry.

The first step is to take a verbal picture of what happened. This discussion ought to be as free from judgments or evaluative descriptors as possible. The intent is to simply and clearly describe what happened—whether it was a rousing success or a dismal failure. This verbal picture becomes a who-did-what-when scenario. The case study method developed by Harvard Business School could be one template to use. Another pattern could be a simple outline of decisions, events, and observable outcomes. The critical aspect here is the willingness to suspend judgment and look at the event in order to compile all the data.

The second step is a conversation about the expected—or unexpected—outcomes. We need to ask ourselves the following questions:

The Learning Process
1. Take a verbal picture of what happened.
2. Have a conversation about the expected—or unexpected—outcomes.
3. Introduce values and judgments.
4. Catalogue the learning.

- *What did we intend to accomplish?*
- *What were our expected or anticipated responses from others—both participants and observers—and ourselves?*
- *How did our experience fulfill, exceed, or fall short of our goals?*

This should be a step in the process where expectations and hopes are simply set aside from the observable outcomes. Try to keep judgment from clouding this descriptive step.

The third step is to introduce values and judgments. Here we move beyond the known facts and begin interjecting our thoughts and feelings about the event. Our questions are:

- *How do we evaluate the event?*
- *Was it a success, a failure, or somewhere in between? Why?*
- *What could we have done differently to ensure our goals were achieved?*
- *Were the right people involved, and was the planning process timely and complete?*

These are some of the questions that begin transforming the experience into a learning opportunity.

At this stage, candor is critical. Set the ground rules early. Let everyone know this isn't a time of personal blame or praise, but it's the point where there can be exchanges of disagreement or passionate agreement! At this stage we ought to expect personal values to enter the conversation. Some people may want the event to be seen in a much better light, while others want to prove that it never should've happened. This step might also include comments by participants or observers—although it isn't necessary. The point is to learn as much as possible from what happened.

The last step in the learning process is to catalogue the learning. By this I mean we need to have a record of our conversations for future reference. It's also important in this step to make sure all of the information from the previous three steps is recorded in some way—notes, tape recording, video, or some other means. This document then serves as a library of our experiences and conclusions, and provides invaluable information for future reference.

This is a simple process but difficult to do at times. (If it were so simple to accomplish, I wouldn't be writing this article.) So why doesn't it happen more often in our ministries? The answer, I believe, is equally simple. We move from one event to another too quickly. We rarely feel the grace of slowing down enough to learn—let alone catalogue—the learning for future reference or to share with someone else.

SETTING THE COURSE

The first requirement for implementing such processes in ministry is that the mind of the leader must change. Leaders will need to accept responsibility for valuing and practicing such a process. The leader as learner is a potent model.

Not long after coming to Prince of Peace church, I had the opportunity for such an experience. I inherited an early Tuesday morning men's Bible study. Attendance was small—12 to 16 men every week. My judgment was that the conversation would be enhanced with more men coming. However, one of the major obstacles for growth was the conference room in which we met, because it held no more than 15 people comfortably. But the regulars valued their "almost one-on-one" time with the senior pastor. Would they give up the intimate space with which they'd become familiar in order for more men to be involved?

With little conversation, we moved into a large atrium. Attendance began to grow, but the loss of intimacy was a problem for some of the men. How could we adapt to a larger space with more men present and still have that necessary connection? I asked colleagues at Prince of Peace, and I didn't accept that it had to be either growth or intimacy—there had to be a win-win solution.

Eventually, someone suggested that we equip the room with round tables that would seat no more than eight men at a time. We'd then shift the Bible study to include small-group conversations at the tables, based upon the lesson taught that morning. An amazing opportunity to learn had presented itself. And I learned more than anyone. Now the solution seems so simple and obvious, but at the time it wasn't either!

So the process was implemented informally. Since then we've used it on a formal basis in our teams after any major event or significant experience. We've decided that the learning is too great to disregard, and we need to be intentional in its implementation.

The process then moved from the leader's mind to the leader's behavior to a cultural value and practice. Now such meetings occur throughout the system. The practice has grown far beyond my abilities to make it happen. And the learnings are abundant. We still haven't provided the library for other leaders that I hope we could—

which reminds me to visit the process on a regular basis with my team. But at least within our ministry teams, the learning—and the sharing of what we learned—occurs on a regular basis.

MOVING BEYOND OUR EXPECTATIONS

I believe there's still one more critical element necessary before our ministries can benefit from such a commitment to learning. We need the spiritual grace to not punish ourselves as leaders for what we don't know. The only thing confusion tells us is that we're finding ourselves in a place we hadn't anticipated! In other words, our prophetic limitations are made known to us.

I believe leaders will be more willing to engage in the learning process if we can set aside our perfectionist expectations of ourselves. The truth of the matter is, you don't know what you don't know...until you know it! I know it sounds silly, but this little mantra of mine has helped me get past my personal guilt about things that haven't happened the way I intended. This frees me up to approach learning openly and with a receptive spirit.

Paul tells us, "And we know that in all things God works for the good of those who love him, who have been called according to his purpose" (Romans 8:28). This is a word of grace for anyone involved in ministry. Paul tells us that we can't anticipate everything that will happen, but that the Holy Spirit will be actively involved in everything for good, for the building of God's kingdom. But we can't see the activity of God on our behalf nor experience God's blessings if we don't take time to reflect upon what's happened. And how able are we to see the work of the Holy Spirit if we can't push past our fear of failure or guilt of imperfection?

Success or failure, joy or sorrow, ease or hardship—all can be instruments of God to teach and grow us. That promise alone is worth taking the time for, isn't it?

TAKING THE FIRST STEP

What are you waiting for? Initiate this basic procedure for your next ministry event.

As you plan your next event, take the time to make sure you put the learning process in place.

Create documentation that will help you evaluate all four steps.

- Event-planning form—location, people involved, target audience, budget.
- Marketing materials—bulletin announcements, flyers.
- Event documentation—audio, video, or multimedia.
- Debriefing forms—questionnaires or evaluation sheets.

When scheduling dates for the event, include a meeting time on the calendar for your leaders to get together after the event as well.

- Gather any information from past events that are similar for comparison.
- Replicate the process.
- Create the process in a way that can be duplicated in other ministry areas.

- Have someone from another ministry area join you in the process in order for them to understand the process.

- Celebrate your accomplishments. Plan a time to celebrate with your ministry team after you've completed the learning process for each event.

THE LEADERSHIP JOURNEY
Being a Pastor Isn't Always What You Expect or Hope It to Be

by DAVID MCQUEEN | *(May/June 2002)*

For 20 years I dreamed of being a lead pastor. And then it happened. I became the lead pastor of Beltway Park Baptist Church in Abilene, Texas, almost four years ago. I felt as if I'd finally stepped into the position I'd been trained for—life was good, until…

…I stood by the side of a 20-year-old widow as she and her two daughters looked for the last time at the face of their husband and father after he was killed in a trucking accident.

…I found one of our church members lying behind the exhaust pipe of her car in a closed garage, attempting suicide.

…I was asked by a church member about divorce because of a unique situation. Her husband had a frontal lobotomy in a last-ditch effort to stop life-threatening seizures. He wasn't expected to survive, but did. However, he's now a completely different person, full of paranoia and fits of raging, abusive anger toward her and her children.

…I prayed (and later counseled) with a young lady who requested I pray that God would make her breasts larger.

…I had to ask people to financially sacrifice to build the building I said I'd never build, but then knew we needed if we were to fulfill God's vision for our church.

...I confronted and led our leadership in church discipline regarding a man leaving his pregnant wife and three children so he could be with a woman he met on the Internet.

My dream position has hit reality, and I'm learning a great deal on the accelerated track. I've asked myself, why did I want to be a pastor?

WHY I CHOSE MINISTRY

I became a Christian when I was 13 years old. I was the spiritual byproduct of a bus ministry that started picking me up in fourth grade. I can't remember wanting to be anything but a pastor since I was 14 years old. From my first visit to church, I thought the person "up front" was the greatest. I knew I wanted to be the up-front person. My denomination really didn't have the language for being "called into ministry," but looking back, I knew I was called.

So I did what called people do—I went to Bible college and seminary. While finishing seminary, I had the opportunity to join the staff of an independent megachurch where I served in various positions for almost nine years. Then four years ago, I became the up-front man of a small, Southern Baptist church in the throes of transition. And though I wouldn't trade positions with anyone, being a lead pastor hasn't always been what I expected it to be. Being relatively young—35-years-old—I realize there's more ahead. But I'd like to highlight two big lessons I've learned so far.

WHO'S IN CONTROL?

I know this sounds basic, but it's one thing to know something in your mind, and a completely different thing to really understand it. I started my training for church leadership during the height of the church growth movement. And though I'm sure I misunderstood and misapplied much of what I heard, I came away believing the goal of leadership was to grow a church, and the means of growing a church was audience knowledge and creative methodology. I really thought if I was educated enough and creative enough, I could be a success at this thing called church.

And then one day it hit me. God was neither in my goals nor my means. Deep down, the reason I was leading a church and the reason I wanted to grow it was for me—for me to feel successful, for me to feel significant, for me to receive glory. Through several events, I felt God teaching me one foundational lesson: This isn't about you, and you can't do this thing called church without me. And then it happened—harsh reality hit me between the eyes.

It was a terrible week. One of the policemen in my church called, giving me the heads up that a fellow member was about to be arrested for trafficking child pornography. When Joe (not his real name) arrived home after making bail, I was waiting for him. Soon his wife walked in, and he began to weep as we watched his arrest on the 6 o'clock news. He swore through his tears he'd never done anything like that.

The next morning a neighbor and longtime friend called Joe's house. The neighbor's family had been watching the news the night before. Later that night, their teenage boys told them Joe had molested them many times when they were younger. The wife called that morning to vent her anger, and the boys' father was on his way over to take care of business. Joe left his house quickly and later that afternoon I stood with his wife as the police told her they found Joe dead from a self-inflicted gunshot wound. Together we told her two sons that their father was gone.

We had the funeral early the next week. In those few days, a large number of boys came forward with the same story about Joe. Some were now young men almost as old as me. Others were still elementary age. In fact, at the funeral one of the pallbearers had been told that morning by his own elementary-age son that Joe had molested him recently. This man was torn between his own anger and his Christlike desire to help Joe's family. To this day I can't remember much of what I said at the funeral.

A couple of days later, the police called me again. They told me the evidence against Joe was overwhelming. None of them had ever been so convinced a man was guilty. Would I tell his wife and children of his guilt? That afternoon, along with her sister, I told this courageous woman that during her marriage of over 20 years, her husband had been living a secret, hideous, evil lie.

Later, in my conversation with God, I told him, "I quit. I didn't sign up for this. I signed up to be the up front leader and to be a success. I don't know how to do this." And I had one of those moments—a time when God spoke directly to my heart. Though I can't remember the exact words, it went something like this: "Good. It's about time you figured that out. It's not about you, your abilities, or your success. It's about me—my power, my name, my glory. Now you have a chance to be a real success."

And as I'm learning this lesson, my definition of success is changing. Success isn't about how many people attend the service or how much they give. Success is about faithfulness to the call of God on my life, faithfully joining him in what he's doing. Success is about his glory, not mine. Success is about his name, not mine. And the amazing thing is that it's much more restful. It isn't always easy, but it's restful. His yoke truly is easy and his burden really is light.

IT'S ABOUT TEAM

Another lesson I've learned is about who gets things done. In the last five years, our denominational church has taken advantage of its autonomous roots and made many changes.

1. The pastor they hired—that's me—never even attended a Southern Baptist church. I grew up in the noninstrumental Churches of Christ and served on the staff of an independent, charismatic church.
2. Our church government changed from congregation-led to elder-led.
3. Our worship style changed from traditional to contemporary.
4. Our ministry focus is shifting from a traditional Sunday school model to a combination small group/training class model.

I've had quite a few people ask me how I led this church to such dramatic and seemingly successful change. The honest answer? I didn't. We did. In fact, I believe the absolute first step to bringing about successful change in a church is making the ministry of the church about "us" and not about a leader.

Five years ago this church was at the point of death. The church started 12 years prior with a bang. They had two services and were growing rapidly. But through a series of events over the past 12 years, the church increasingly struggled and spiraled in decline. Both pastors who served during the first 12 years left church ministry after serving this church. Attendance and finances declined. In fact, soon after the second pastor left, the leaders discussed closing the doors and selling the assets.

But then something happened. The people began to cry out to God. They repented for their behavior of letting the pastor do everything. They repented of doing church the way they'd always done it. And they asked God to change them so he could lead this church to become what he designed it to be.

These lay leaders called an interim pastor who began to empower them to be the leaders God called them to be. And they began calling the rest of the people in the church to pray and become a part of the ministry of this fellowship—not just spectators. They began to initiate God-led change. By the time they interviewed my wife and me for the lead pastor role, they made it very clear they wanted a lead pastor, not a one-man show. They wanted a leader truly committed to the "priesthood and ministry of all believers."

And though I still don't like to admit it, I found myself struggling with the idea of actually doing team leadership, of empowering and releasing nonstaff personnel in a radical way to leadership. I always said I believed it. I even encouraged the church where I served on staff to increase its idea of team leadership. But now it was "my" church and "my" success at stake—which takes me back to the question: Who's in control? It was now time, as we like to say here in west Texas, to "put up or shut up."

And for the last four years we've wrestled to "put up." I'll admit, it's not the easiest way to do church. Change occurs more slowly—but it actually happens in a positive way and unity is built. Things aren't always done the way I want them done. In the old paradigm, it's easier to do it yourself or hire staff. But the results of doing it through team ministry far outweigh the alternatives. I see the people in our congregation sacrificing, growing, and understanding what it means to catch God's heart for people as they serve them. And I've seen the ministry expand far beyond what I could imagine because it's about us, not me.

THE JOURNEY CONTINUES

My dream position hit reality somewhere in the last four years, and I wanted to quit. But in the midst of wanting to quit, God touched my heart and changed the very core of who I am in regards to leading a church. And the amazing thing is, I serve and lead with more joy, security, and power than I ever thought possible. In the midst of the harsh realities of serving people in a broken world, I can't imagine doing anything else.

In this journey I continue to learn what it means to be a lead pastor—mostly from the mistakes I make. But the most important lessons I'm learning have to do with the heart. I believe all of us in full-time ministry, whether we're the lead pastor or serve in an equally important role as a staff member, must continually let God fashion our hearts. Jesus said it's from the "overflow of the heart" that we speak and lead. Leadership is ultimately about who we are in him, allowing him to overflow through our hearts to a church and a world in desperate need of him.

I can't wait—or maybe I can—to see what I'm going to learn in the next four years.

PINPOINTING YOUR LEADERSHIP FORTE

by ROBERT JOHNSON | *(July/August 2005)*

One of my favorite stories about leadership is of a particular situation during a denominational meeting in which there was an attempt to oust the top leader.

During the week of the convention, there were behind-the-scenes political moves, macabre meetings, and secretive strategic gatherings. Late into the convention, it was the majority opinion that the leader's dismissal was all but done. But on the last day of the convention, the leader—not alarmed at all by the sideline opinion polls and being absent from all of the strategizing—took to the lectern and preached his annual address. The response to his message was so overwhelming that it cancelled the need to even take a vote. Not only did he remain in office, he continued as the leader for another decade! He used his leadership forte of rising above the muck of denominational politics. He's a perfect example of a leader who understood his leadership forte and used it effectively.

Know your leadership forte. Every leader has a forte, and effective leadership requires knowing your forte and using it in the right place and at the right time. The leadership forte is not the same as your set of leadership skills.

Your leadership forte is the thing that makes all of your leadership skills relevant and productive.

The forte of presence. For example, some leaders have great presence. They can walk into a room and their very presence evokes energy, excitement, and commitment to a vision. Too much presence would dilute the power of this forte, but presence at the critical, "turning point" moments can claim a victory!

The forte of humor. Other leaders have the forte of great humor. They have a knack for breaking through tension, adversity, and antagonism with timely jest. While humor is rarely mentioned in business books as a key leadership skill, leaders whose forte is humor could not survive without it. That's how they get things done. They make people laugh, and through the laughter, people are healed, united, relaxed, inspired, and energized for action.

Here's the question to help you discover your leadership forte: "When the pressure's on and the stakes are high, what do you do to keep a vision moving forward?"

PLUNGE INTO PROFESSIONAL ADVICE

"Effective ministry depends upon talented, capable church leaders. But a leader who burns the candle at both ends will soon burn out entirely."

—D. MICHAEL LINDSAY

(March/April 2006, pg. 40)

A PASTOR'S MANY HATS

What Does Your Congregation Want in a Leader?

by DEAN RIDINGS | *(March/April 1998)*

One Saturday morning, a dozen people held a carwash in Reston, a booming northern Virginia suburb of Washington, D.C. They wanted to serve the community "to show the love of Christ."

They picked a spot on a main artery in town. A couple of the participants held up signs inviting folks to pull in, and many did. Dirt was washed away as car and van owners ate doughnuts, sipped coffee, and chatted with each other and the workers.

The car washers didn't take donations; instead they prayed for the drivers as they pulled back into the flow and fray of life in D.C.

It was all in a day's work, for the 12 were pastors—black, white, from diverse Christian churches—with the common hope of showing people in a practical way that God loves them and pastors do too.

One of the pastors who scrubbed and hosed down cars that day was Mike Minter of Reston Bible Church. His vision for reaching the community of Reston for Christ is one of the biggest reasons church members Terry and Sharon White appreciate him. Minter's vision began when he realized there should be a greater unity among (and modeled by) the community's pastors. He found pastors from various denominational backgrounds both receptive and thirsty for regular meetings.

"These pastors began meeting several years ago to pray for the church in Reston," says Terry, communications vice president with Prison Fellowship Ministries. "Now they meet monthly as a group and weekly in sub-groups to pray.

"On several occasions, the pastors have taken overnight retreats together where they were able to express and share with each other some of their joys and their deep hurts and discouragements in the ministry."

In addition to "unity in diversity," people in the pews appreciate the fact that their pastors aren't "lone rangers" in ministry and life. Individuals across the nation—from various backgrounds and churches—identified the following marks of appreciated pastors.

THEY PREACH GOD'S WORD

Lloyd Mattson and his wife, Elsie, have been in Christian ministry for many years. Though their work often keeps them on the road, they believe it's important to have a "home church." They chose Bayside Baptist Church in Superior, Wisconsin, primarily because of the preaching of Len Carlson, who has served the congregation for some 20 years.

"Our souls were nourished by the messages and ministry of the people," says Lloyd. "But the preaching was the determining factor. Len's preaching is usually topical and textual; his sermons are simple, direct, honest, unequivocal, biblical, and brief."

Lloyd adds, "Our pastor is a humble man of God with remarkable insights and a gentle spirit. He exemplifies speaking the truth in love. He never avoids issues—abortion, homosexuality, divorce, alcohol abuse, sex—yet he's unabrasive, kind."

Regarding Reston Bible Church's Mike Minter, Terry White says, "Mike's strong adherence to the biblical text, fleshed out with practical applications, and delivered with a rapier wit and self-deprecating style, make every sermon a treat. While he's entertaining, he never fails to deliver a biblical message of substance, and he has no fear about attacking real issues.

"Much of the reason for Mike's appeal—and for the church's growth—is his use of Scripture. Though he doesn't get harsh, and doesn't 'guilt' people, he does speak the truth, even when it's hard."

THEY'RE "REAL"

Bruce and Rita McIntosh and their young family attend Walnut Creek Presbyterian Church in a small bedroom community not far from the heart of San Francisco. The same day the McIntoshes arrived four years ago, the church welcomed Pastor John Westfall. Bruce and Rita say one of the main reasons they stayed—and why they appreciate Westfall so much—is because he's authentic.

"In order for the people in our Homebuilders Sunday school class to get to know him and his wife better, we held a dinner party," says Bruce, a lawyer in the Bay area. "During the course of the discussion, he told us how he was picked to be the pastor. He had visited the church and decided it wasn't the right match.

He said he tried to 'talk them out of it' when the church gave him the call."

Bruce continues: "Later that evening, he opened up about his personal life. He shared that he has been married for 25 years and has spent most of it in marriage counseling."

"He doesn't put on airs," adds Rita, "and pretend that he's better or more spiritual than everyone else. He admits his unfaithful attitudes and brings us and himself to the Lord."

Rita recalls how, on one particular Sunday, their pastor was open about his personal struggle to preach about tithing. "On stewardship Sunday he would always conveniently be out of town or have someone else preach, anything to get out of it. He shared how over the course of time some pastor friends of his convinced him that people's monetary giving was a sign of their spiritual health and, therefore, he should concern himself with it."

Rita says that their pastor went on "to challenge people to give—of their money as well as time and talents—but said that if people are giving anywhere near 10 percent of their income he feels sorry for them because they must be near poverty."

"When he preaches his sermons," concludes Bruce, "Westfall says, 'Jesus talks to all of us—even me.' I appreciate the fact that the Bible talks to him, too."

THEY HAVE CARING HEARTS

Irv Lee, a squadron commander at the Air Force Academy in Colorado Springs, Colorado, his wife, Chandra, and their two young children attend Woodmen Valley Chapel—recently named one of the fastest-growing churches in the United States. The Lees believe a major reason for the church's growth is that Pastor Jim Tomberlin "effectively communicates and demonstrates God's heart."

"Our pastor really has a caring heart and shows this through the ministries we have to reach out and meet the needs of diverse people who attend our church," says Chandra. "We have special parking places for single moms, and visitors can flash their lights and get directed to convenient parking spaces by people in our parking ministry."

"Pastor Jim is very articulate and communicates the gospel clearly and with cultural relevancy," says Irv. "He personally led a meeting with minority members of our congregation and others who shared his interest in finding ways to help make the church more sensitive to minorities. As a result, church and ministry leaders are more aware of culturally sensitive biases that are sometimes innocently communicated, and they try to ensure considerations are made to avoid cultural insensitivity."

Carl Lundstrom and his wife, Kay, have been members of First Baptist Church in Elgin, Illinois, for 36 years. Owner of Lundstrom Insurance and a prominent leader in his church and the Christian community at large, Carl appreciated their pastor, Willie Reed (who passed away last summer), because of the ways he would reflect Jesus' love and care in the church and community.

"Willie reached out when people were hurting—especially when they were in the hospital, dealing with deaths, accidents, and so forth," says Carl. "Willie was at the hospital bedside with my mother, my wife, and me when my father died."

Carl notes that people value pastors like Willie, who are "true to God's Word and share it openly and regularly from the pulpit, and pastors who shepherd the church attendee into a relationship with Christ."

THEY SHARE THE MINISTRY

"Mike in no way tries to do it all," says Reston Bible's Terry White. "He freely gives away large parts of what is traditionally the senior pastor's turf, including having other pastors and lay people lead communion, conduct baptisms, and do virtually all other parts of the ministry." At Woodmen Valley Chapel, Pastor Jim doesn't feel that he has to do it all, either. In fact, he regularly turns over the pulpit to a fellow staff pastor or elder, and Christian leaders from the many parachurch groups in Colorado Springs.

In addition, he takes seriously his call to "prepare God's people for works of service" (Ephesians 4:11-12), and chal-lenges each member to get plugged into the right ministry fit by discovering his or her God-given passions, personality style, gifts, talents, and abilities.

"Pastor Jim actively encourages and empowers members of our church to use their spiritual gifts with other local fellowships and Christian ministries," adds Irv Lee.

At Walnut Creek Presbyterian Church, John Westfall likes to "keep the pot boiling," says Bruce McIntosh, "with new programs, new things, and fresh ideas." The McIntoshes have helped initiate adult and children's ministries, and served on the committee to develop the

"Called to Serve Ministries"—again, to help match spiritual gifts and personal abilities with ministries within and outside the church.

"It's important for pastors to give away the ministry to the congregation," says Rita McIntosh, "and that means they'll not necessarily do all the same functions they once might have done, yet [those functions] will still be covered by the body."

THEY HANDLE ISSUES APPROPRIATELY

What's a pastor to do when someone in the pews stands up and takes issue with a sermon point? Lloyd Mattson shares a time when that happened with Pastor Len at Bayside Baptist Church, and how he appreciated the pastor's appropriate response.

"One Sunday morning, a woman—a stranger—interrupted the sermon, rising to her feet and insisting in a loud voice that she be allowed to speak to a point of disagreement," Lloyd says. "Len paused and quietly offered to meet with her later, but said, with a touch of humor, 'This is my time.'

"The woman persisted, but Len did not raise his voice. He kept assuring her he would hear her later, but not now. When she would not yield, a member of the congregation launched into 'Amazing Grace,' others joined in, and the woman stalked out.

"Len continued with the wry comment, 'I always wondered what I would do if this ever happened. Now I know!' "

At Walnut Creek Presbyterian, Pastor John's responses aren't subtle. Says Bruce McIntosh: "In response to negative letters, he says there are times he sends back maps to other churches letting them know where they might be better suited.

"He gets a lot of unsigned letters. He got an e-mail, and said, 'The great thing about e-mail is that, even though it's unsigned, you can still reply to the sender.' "

THEY SEEK RECONCILIATION

At Woodmen Valley Chapel, says Irv Lee, "Pastor Jim is open to assisting and learning from pastors of different denominations to advance the kingdom of God in Colorado Springs."

Pastor Jim and Calvin Johnson—pastor of the local African-American congregation Solid Rock Christian Church—have formed a partnership so members of both churches will minister together as well as support, learn from, and encourage one another.

At Bayside Baptist Church in Superior, Wisconsin, Pastor Len is also concerned about racial and denominational reconciliation. "He participates aggressively in interdenominational activities, respecting leaders even if he disagrees with them theologically," says Lloyd Mattson.

Several months ago at Reston Bible Church, the dozen or so pastors whom Mike Minter called together held a combined worship service. Terry White says that nearly 700 attended the evening of praise, worship, prayer, repentance, and racial reconciliation.

"The Messianic Jewish pastor blew the shofar to start the service, a band and group of singers from one of the charismatic black churches led the music, and all the pastors participated in leading various parts of the service," says Terry. "It was a remarkable demonstration of the 'minimization of differences' among very diverse congregations."

Terry adds, "That night, I think we experienced a bit of what heaven will be like, with all colors and flavors of Christians worshiping together. Yet there was repentance for personal, corporate, and national wrongdoing, and a great concern exhibited for our neighbors and co-workers who do not yet know the Lord."

Terry appreciated the resounding impact of the service as well as his pastor's humility in it all. "Mike hosted the event in our church," he says, "because it's the biggest facility of the churches represented and the meeting was his idea. But he in no way dominated it, and he didn't lead it; he just participated as one of the pastors."

What are people in the pews looking for in a pastor? "I think most people want a model of the faith and integrity they hear about in sermons," Lloyd Mattson sums up. "They need to sense the love of God in the person of God."

OPINIONS COUNT!

Feedback from your congregation about how you're measuring up as a pastor doesn't have to be scary. Copy these questions, distribute the questionnaire following your worship service, and provide a convenient place for them to be returned. Ask for honest input, and assure your congregation that their answers are anonymous.

1. What one thing do you wish Pastor _____ would do that he isn't doing now?

2. What one thing do you wish Pastor _____ would stop doing that he does now?

3. What one thing do you hope Pastor _____ never stops doing?

4. What one thing does Pastor _____ do now that needs improvement? Do you have any suggestions for how to improve that area?

Permission to copy this box from *REV! Magazine's Bathroom Guide to Leadership* granted for local church use. Copyright © 2007 Group Publishing, Inc., P.O. Box 481, Loveland, CO 80539. www.group.com

THE PERFECT STAFF AND LEADER

by ALAN NELSON | *(January/February 2004)*

How to find the perfect staff or ministry team member:

How to find the perfect ministry leader:

"Bear with each other and forgive whatever grievances you may have against one another" (Colossians 3:13).

Peter Drucker said in effect that the purpose of an organization is to render our weaknesses useless. Vibrant ministries focus on team member strengths, while bearing with each other's weak spots. Although inadequacies can't be overlooked when they tear at the ministry fabric or they diminish strengths, the idea of finding the perfect pastor, staff, or team member is hopelessly flawed.

Whenever you work shoulder-to-shoulder with others, you quickly discern each other's shortcomings. By leaning on our limps, we'll render each other lame. Leaders must keep the team's focus on individual strengths. Grace isn't an excuse for enduring dysfunction, but it certainly makes a ministry environment both realistic and a great spiritual setting for authentic community.

Enough said.

PIONEERING CHANGE AS CHURCH LEADERS

by HANS FINZEL | *(July/August 2004)*

My ankles were wrenching painfully against old, rock-hard dirt ruts. Burning wind sliced across a barrage of prairie grass and straight through my flimsy cotton shirt. Overhead, a blistering Midwest sun made a mockery of the straw hat I'd worn to ward off its rays. Next to me, my wife and children were actually laughing, enjoying themselves. And to be honest, despite my discomfort, so was I.

The year was 1993, and America was celebrating the 150th anniversary of the Oregon Trail. Seized by an oddly ambitious curiosity, the Finzel bunch piled into a motor home and set out to follow the old path along its entire route, learning its history and its lessons.

We learned that the Oregon Trail stretches some 2,000 miles—half of the width of the United States—from Independence, Missouri, to Oregon City, Oregon. At both ends of the trail and all along the route lay informative interpretive centers where we soon learned of the many who tried and the many who died.

Of the 6,000 people who set out between 1843 and 1846, 1,000 died along the way. Yet tales of hardship didn't deter these early pioneers who settled the Pacific Northwest.

"What's wrong with you people?" "Why didn't you quit?" The questions never let up. They only grew louder as our family trail wound on. Our air-conditioned motor home stood ready for us nearby; theirs was a Conestoga wagon with wooden wheels and no indoor plumbing. "Why did they do it?" "Would we have gone along?"

In the middle of my misery, I started to picture being somewhere else. Hawaii. Alaska. Even the Hampton Inn in the next town over—anywhere but here. And that's when it struck me.

They were dreamers!

Their minds weren't showing them this baked-out oven. They were focused on swimming images of Oregon! Of lush green valleys and rows of Douglas firs lining the banks of the Willamette.

Churches in decline today desperately need the eyes of dreamers. Solutions lie not in focusing on the rocks in the path, but on the possibilities ahead. "The real voyage of discovery consists not in seeking new landscapes but in having new eyes," says Marcel Proust. The eyes of a dreamer.

DREAMING AND THE SEIZING OF RISK

I see two kinds of churches on our North American landscape today: dying churches and changing churches. If you're not changing, you're probably dying. As I travel and speak in many churches, I see so many declining churches that are paralyzed by fear and held captive by a few long-time power people that hold the church hostage. I recently spoke in such a church. The pastor poured out his heart to me about the few big giving families in the church that are withholding their money to show that they don't condone the changes he's making. My advice to him was this: "Lay down the ultimatum. Go for broke with your changes,

despite these obstructionists, or leave the church." It was sad to see the dreams robbed from this young pastor.

Today's churches need courageous dreamers and pioneers that will make the church work for the world of 2004 and beyond. We desperately need visionaries that can lead our churches into a vital future of ministry that meets the spiritual needs of today's world.

If you weren't a dreamer—even a latent one, whose dreamer potential lay buried under layers of adult cares—you'd be incapable of boarding a wagon for the West in the 1800s.

That brings me to the other germane fact about the Oregon Trail pioneers: They were risk-takers. I truly believe the two quali-ties—dreaming and risk-taking—are totally intertwined. Very few people have the intestinal fortitude to take risks (at least the kind of mammoth risks necessary to make a real difference in this world) without possessing the ability to fantasize a desirable destination. "Do not follow where the path may lead. Go instead where there is no path and leave a trail," says Renn Zaphiropoulos, former presi-dent and CEO of Versatec, Inc.

Business leader Peter Drucker says this about living with risk-takers in our organizations: Every organization needs risk-takers, to discover...

1. Risks you can afford to take.

2. Risks you cannot afford to take.

3. Risks you cannot afford not to take.

Maybe not everyone was cut out for the Oregon Trail. But creativity and risk-taking in our churches today aren't just for the gifted few. They're a necessary component of every learning organization. Your church needs risk-takers at every level.

WHY CHANGE?

Most people resist change. They prefer the certainty of their misery rather than the misery of uncertainty. Established church members question the need for change. Older, established churches are often very hard to change. But change they must. Henry Kissinger states well the danger of holding back the pioneers that will bring us into the future: "For any student of history, change is the law of life. Any attempt to contain it guarantees an explosion down the road; the more rigid the adherence to the status quo, the more violent the ultimate outcome will be." If we hold back the changes needed in our churches, they'll either explode into divisions or die.

I have to address the fundamental question some of you may be

WHY CHANGE OUR CHURCH?

- God's stirring a new thing
- A sense of urgency
- Changing audience
- Changing workers
- Changing demographics
- Changing marketplace
- Lack of clear goals
- Financial failure
- Lack of vision
- Ineffectiveness
- Repeated failure
- Plateaued ministry
- Declining impact
- High attrition rates
- Confusion over leadership roles
- Low morale
- Flat-out failure

asking: "Why change our churches?" There are so many reasons, that I've developed the following list as a sampling of the big issues.

INVENTING THE NEXT VELCRO FOR YOUR CHURCH

The #1 skill necessary for exhuming and then honing your individual creativity is to learn how to think associatively. What does that mean? It means abandoning the linear model of Western thinking, first of all. Am I leading us down a path of Eastern mysticism? Not really. But I do think we can learn something from cultures that refuse to think of life in terms of straight lines stretching from Point A to Point B. We can benefit from picturing it instead, if only temporarily, as a series of circles, or even meandering paths, which not only intertwine but educate each other.

Again, I'm not going to launch into instructions for the lotus position or the latest trendy form of yoga. But I will say that when you start free-associating in a nonlinear manner, you allow parts of your thinking to latch onto others they might never have approached before. That's when you enter the zone where true genius is possible. Instead of B following A, it might follow T. And "B after T" might spark innovations and ramifications no one ever expected—the kind of "eurekas" that change organizations, and our world, forever.

Try getting your church leaders together and visualizing a better way. Give permission for dreaming. When was the last time your church leaders got together with a blank white board to dream about the future? Do you allow any ideas to go on the board, no matter how off-the-wall or out-of-the-box? That's what it takes to come up with the creative ideas that will take your congregation to a vibrant future.

When Robert Schuller began the Crystal Cathedral in a drive-in theater in Garden Grove, California, it was the last of 100 other ideas that didn't work. People called him crazy—but it worked.

How safe is it to be a dreamer in your group? Is change rewarded or is preserving the rituals of tradition?

If tradition is your mantra, you'd better get to work.

CAN COFFEE INSTRUCT THE CHURCH?

When Starbucks came along, I became their perfect customer. My wife, Donna, and I grab Starbucks lattes together nearly every afternoon after work so we can catch up on our day. We have our own table, and they know us on a first-name basis!

Years ago, when Howard Schultz bought the Starbucks franchise and began to dream about bringing the European café culture to America, countless skeptics and critics scoffed. "No American will ever pay more than a dollar for a cup of coffee!" He proved them massively wrong. Everywhere I go, not only in the United States, but also around the world, I see that familiar green-and-white disk.

It's a lot more than coffee. Howard Schultz actually changed the habits of modern America. What he'd seen in the streets of Naples he grafted into his home culture. Schultz tells how in his book *Pour Your Heart Into It* (Hyperion Press). I love the four principles upon which he operates as a coffee evangelist:

- *Care more than others think wise.*
- *Risk more than others think safe.*
- *Dream more than others think practical.*
- *Expect more than others think possible.*

I have a pastor friend in California who applied lessons learned from Starbucks to build a beautiful outdoor plaza between their church buildings with a full-service espresso bar for members to enjoy between services. It's a huge hit at keeping people on campus and stimulating fellowship.

Our message of the saving grace of Jesus Christ is worth so much more than a cup of coffee. Let's learn the lesson of change and throw the same creativity and passion into our efforts.

CAUTION: DON'T KILL THE DREAMERS

Are you killing the best dreams of others, which will bring you the future? Are others killing your dreams for your church?

In my book *The Top 10 Mistakes Leaders Make* (David C. Cook Publishing), I have a whole chapter on making room for mavericks. Here are a few observations about how to kill dreamers.

> The three deadliest phrases for the maverick are:
> 1. We tried that before and it didn't work.
> 2. We've always done it that way.
> 3. We've never done it that way.

I also have in that book what I call the "11 Commandments of

Organizational Paralysis," or "How to put people in their place if they try to bring us into the future with their great new ideas." Here are some of their statements:

"That's impossible."
"We don't do things that way around here."
"We've never done it that way."
"It's too radical a change for us."
"We tried something like that before and it didn't work."
"I wish it were that easy."
"It's against policy to do it that way."
"When you've been around a little longer, you'll understand."
"Who gave you permission to change the rules?"
"Let's get real, OK?"
"How dare you suggest that what we're doing is wrong!"

Not only are dreamers essential to a church's survival, but each of us is a dreamer-in-training. If you're not one, get on the ball and quick. In today's radically changing world, we need church leaders who allow nonlinear thinking and dreamers to help them survive.

HIRE CALLING
How to Find the Right Person for the Job

by PAUL KRAUSE | *(July/August 2000)*

Nothing's worse than hiring the wrong person. Except maybe hiring the wrong person for the wrong job again and again, causing constant turnover and plunging morale. But with the right person in the right job, ministry can run smoothly and happily for everyone involved. The right candidates are out there somewhere—how can you find them? It's not an easy process, but finding someone who's a perfect fit with your church more than makes up for the extra time it takes to do a thorough job.

Finding the right staff members requires church leaders to consider the candidates' spiritual lives, their work experiences, and their interests. I like the metaphor of an airport runway. At night, a pilot knows that he or she has a good approach angle and trajectory when all the lights of the runway are aligned. These lights provide a clear signal to the pilot that the plane is lined up for a safe landing. I believe that there are "runway lights" in the staff selection process as well. When we hire employees at Willow Creek Community Church, we discuss five essential runway lights which should align during the hiring process: affirmed calling, prepared lifestyle, seasoned spirituality, demonstrated service, and matched talents with the position.

AFFIRMED CALLING

Candidates often say, "God is calling me to this position." This places the leader in a hard spot; after all, who wants to resist God's will? I'm certain, however, that just as God leads individuals to pursue vocational ministry, he affirms that calling through the leadership of local churches, just as he did with the church in Acts 6.

Questions to ask regarding calling:

1. Tell me about your spiritual journey. How does this position fit with God's work in your life?
2. Where have you seen God working in this type of position?
3. What interested you in applying at our church and for this particular position?

PREPARED LIFESTYLE

Vocational ministry entails more than employment; it has significant implications on a person's entire lifestyle. It's essential that the candidate be prepared for the implications of the lifestyle that accompanies church employment. The financial impact alone requires great attention and preparation. Salaries in churches (and all nonprofits, for that matter) are significantly less than wages in comparable marketplace positions. Frequently a candidate enthused about vocational ministry will need to continue in a higher salary marketplace position until they can "get their financial house in order." Good budget counseling should be pursued before a person enters ministry to ensure that the lower wages don't create unnecessary frustration or distraction down the road.

A second lifestyle question concerns evening and weekend responsibilities. A staff member's job responsibilities often call for them to develop, shepherd, or lead lay people who are most available on weekends and in the evenings. Candidates should be told about these responsibilities and have opportunity to discuss any reservations before signing on.

A third lifestyle question centers around the role of staff to model a spiritual life and church involvement for others. We use the phrase, "Is the life you're inviting others to live the life you're living yourself?" Many new church employees are unaware of the visibility that accompanies a staff position. People look to the church staff to gauge what the Christian life looks like and how to pursue involvement in the church. This may exert unexpected pressure on spouses and families and could lead to frustration about "working where you worship."

Questions to determine lifestyle preparation:

1. The salary range for this position is $_____ to $_____.
   Are you prepared to accept a position in that range?
2. This position involves work during the evenings and weekends. What questions do you have about evening and weekend work activities?
3. What will be challenging about working where you worship?

SEASONED SPIRITUALITY

Churches need spiritually maturing Christ-followers to contribute in all areas of church ministry, whether pastoral care, administration, or support. The need for spiritually seasoned employees has two critical expressions—proven character and spiritual "self-feeders."

The first seems obvious; You can't train character. The second point is less obvious. The demands and pace of ministry are great. The staff needs to be able to refresh themselves spiritually through spiritual disciplines—we call these people spiritual self-feeders. Often candidates expect that working on a church staff will turbo-boost their spiritual lives. They hope that being in a spiritual environment will help them grow, perhaps by osmosis. The need for authentic servants in our churches requires that candidates demonstrate an ability to walk with God through a variety of seasons.

Questions to discover spiritual readiness:

1. Describe how you're presently nurturing your spiritual growth through Christian disciplines on your own.

2. In your pursuit of becoming more Christlike, what areas are most difficult for you and need the most attention?

3. Describe a time when you experienced conflict in your past position. Describe the circumstances leading up to it and the actions you took to resolve the situation.

4. What has been your greatest source of frustration in previous positions?

DEMONSTRATED SERVICE

It's important that staff members have experience as volunteer contributors in a local church to have their spiritual gifts affirmed.

This allows them to develop a servant spirit, a desire to give of themselves to God's work, and a sense of the challenges of ministry. They will also see that dealing with others' spiritual and personal struggles can deplete a servant's energy. Has the person learned to depend on God for his strength as he serves?

A potential staff member would also see that decision-making processes in churches are often different from the marketplace, with many more ministry decisions being made by consensus rather than by relying on one person's judgment exclusively.

Questions regarding service:

1. What ministries have you been involved with and in what capacity?
2. What were the most challenging aspects of that ministry? What was most rewarding?
3. What do you suppose it's like to work here at this church [culture, work atmosphere, and so on]?

MATCHED TALENTS

A church leader enters into a risky situation when he or she tries to shoehorn a candidate into a position. Instead, we should always begin with a clear idea of the position, and then look for people who match that position well. A clear job description is the cornerstone of all aspects of the employment relationship: selection, training, performance management, and even compensation. A good job description answers the following questions: How does this position fit with the church's overall mission? What are the expectations and responsibilities of this position? What specific activities lead to success for this position? What does the ideal candidate possess [in terms of education, work and volunteer experience, spiritual gifts and talents]?

Questions to determine position/talent match:

1. Describe your ideal job.

2. One of the questions I'll ask your last supervisor during a reference check is what your greatest strengths are. What do you think he or she will say? In what areas would he or she say you need to improve?

3. Do you prefer working independently or as part of a team? If you could divide your time between people and tasks, how would you divide that time?

4. If you could only accomplish three things in the next one to five years, what would you accomplish?

5. If you could do anything you wanted—God told you that you were free to choose; you had all the time, money, and education you needed; and you knew for certain that you would succeed—what would you do?

OTHER ISSUES TO CONSIDER

Reference checks are critical. I always say, "Sue is considering employment at our church. Does it surprise you that she would work for a church?" The answer tells me how actively the candidate expressed his or her beliefs at the current workplace.

Also describe the basics about the position and your church's mission (and the need for the staff to be above reproach in all areas). Then ask whether there's anything about the candidate's background or work style that makes the reference wonder about the candidate's fit for the position or the church.

WHAT TO AVOID

Avoid people looking to escape the pressures of the marketplace, those tired of working with non-Christians, or people disgusted by the lifestyles of their coworkers. First, sinners are supposed to sin. God's placed the majority of us in marketplace positions expressly so that we can be salt and light. Second, no church work environment is perfect. Personal relationships, even among God's people, can be strained and difficult. I find that the pressures of the church work environment are disillusioning to those escaping the negative dynamics of the marketplace. Also avoid people assuming that the work experience will be one big small group.

My hope for all church staff members is to see them abide and abound in their work—to abide in the love and life of Jesus Christ (John 15), and to abound in the work of the Lord (1 Corinthians 15:58). If you follow the runway lights during the hiring process, you can bring the right candidate in for a smooth landing at your church.

THE CHURCH @ WORK
Helping Christ-Followers Reach Out in Their Workplace

by JOHN MAXWELL,
STEPHEN GRAVES,
and THOMAS ADDINGTON

(September/October 2005)

The Chicago meeting brought together about 30 followers of Christ, who also happened to be successful, business leaders. They had flown in to pursue a greater understanding of servant leadership. As the meeting progressed, an interesting pattern developed. Whenever the talk focused on business, these leaders dove in with full force and great confidence. They talked about market trends, management theories, branding, and strategic analysis. They reeled off business data the way baseball fanatics quote the batting averages of their favorite players.

When the talk turned to theology or Scripture, however, these well-educated, business-savvy leaders invariably prefaced everything they said with an apology: "I'm not a theologian," they would say, "but I think..." or "I'm not a professional pastor, but it seems like..." When it was time to talk about business, they eagerly explained what they knew. But when the time came to talk about God, they hesitated to even venture what they thought.

Why would otherwise confident business leaders hedge their

statements about their faith, which they all said was the most important area of their lives? For most of them, it wasn't biblical competency but confidence that they lacked. These marketplace leaders did not feel equipped to make a spiritual assertion about their work. They are called as priests to their daily world, yet they stammered when it came time to say, "Thus saith the Lord..." about business.

Have you ever been to physical therapists who did an arm-resistance test? They have you hold both arms straight out from your side. They then push down on each arm one at a time while you push back up in resistance. If one side is weaker than the other in its pushback, it's a sign of spinal misalignment. Similarly, the business leaders in Chicago had a weak "pushback" on the faith side of their lives. This, too, is an alignment problem. If they saw their work and their faith aligned, both sides would be equally confident.

GOD'S CALL TO A "VERY, VERY" LIFE

Scripture calls us to be "very, very" men and women. We're called to be very Bible and very business. Many Christ-followers we meet are either "very business, sort of Bible" or "sort of business, very Bible." A "very, very" person is one who consistently develops a growing expertise in both Bible and business. Being genuinely successful is all about exploring and understanding a "very, very" secular world and becoming a "very, very" disciple with both confidence and credibility.

New believers are the only people with a legitimate reason to say, "I don't know the Bible very well." All others who've been in the faith for a few years ought to know the Book, regardless of whether they receive a paycheck from a church or have attended seminary. Accountants should know Numbers as well as they know numbers. Attorneys should know Judges as well as they know judges. And politicians should know 1 and 2 Kings as well as they know legislative kingpins.

As followers of the incarnate Son of God, Son of Man, how could we aim for less? Jesus was "very, very." He was very human—and very divine. When people try to make him only one or the other, they violate good biblical theology and end up attempting to create a "schizoid" Jesus.

Business people aren't the only ones to sometimes miss the mark of a "very, very" understanding of world and church. Go to any pastors' conference in the country and you'll likely find the opposite side of the coin. You'll find men and women who speak with passion and authority about the Bible, but who hem and haw about the world of work. The world of the church must reacquaint itself with the world of work, for it's here that it has perhaps its largest untapped field of ministry.

We live in a "new economy." Its constantly changing realities have created a heightened sense of insecurity and uncertainty across the entire workforce. The idea of unlimited consumer prosperity is gone. Today people find themselves treading water alone in a global shark-infested ocean. This intersection of a cultural hunger and a biblical mandate has created an unprecedented opportunity for ministry. To be an effective agent of salt and light in this changing chaotic context, a follower of Christ needs to embody a "very, very" mind-set and a "very, very" lifestyle—a person firmly planted in professional excellence and deeply rooted in biblical truth.

The workplace is where the contest over many of today's life issues is being held. When we walk up to the plate, we better have our swing ready. We better be able to hit well and run fast. As men and women who long to represent Christ to the world, we must strive to become "very, very." The church is our dugout, but work is the arena filled with watching, hungry fans where God has called us to play the game.

ONE LAMB ROARING IN A DEN OF LIONS

Bob Briner, our late friend and the longtime president of ProServ Television, came face to face with the difficult nature of this task. From humble beginnings, Bob made his way through the ranks of the highly competitive world of professional sports, working in the front office of the Miami Dolphins before launching a career as an agent and then as a television producer. He was a "player" and he was in the game, but he found himself woefully unprepared to integrate his faith in Jesus with his work.

"As I searched for help in combining Christian living with my world of professional sports and television, it didn't come from my church or denomination," Briner wrote in *Roaring Lambs*, a groundbreaking book challenging believers to impact culture through their work. "And in fairness to this great group of believers, I have not found much help in this area from any of the other traditional evangelical groups."

Briner set out to become a "very, very" person by infiltrating the cultural citadel of media through his work. As an influential force in the world of professional sports, television, and business, he intentionally melded the world of Scripture with the world of daily living, and he did it in a profession that's not exactly known for its overwhelming acceptance of believers in Jesus.

His passions included a strong concern that nonbelievers see Jesus in everything we do, especially the skill and excellence of our work. When he met with the shah of Iran, he wanted to evidence Christ. When he negotiated with Akio Morita, the founder of Sony, he wanted to represent Christ. Bob called that being a "roaring lamb."

SHEPHERDING ROARING LAMBS

Bob found that his church was as ill-equipped as he was to meet this challenge. While schools and professional associates trained him well to excel in his work, he didn't find much training on how to be a follower of Jesus in it—unless he wanted to become a pastor or a missionary. Further, to even take advantage of these biblical training resources, he would have to pack up and move to what he called the "Christian ghetto." Even the best seminary education, however, would have little to teach him about what it means to incarnate Christ in the marketplace.

The church, as we currently know it, is simply not designed to equip believers like Bob to steward their lives at work. For too long the church has operated as a nursing home and not as a boot camp.

In a nursing home, people move in, but they never move out. In a boot camp, you are trained to move out every day, to hit the deck running.

The winds of change, however, are shifting. The church's mission is no longer only about Unchurched Harry and Sally—it's also about Unconnected and Unfulfilled Charlie and Charlene in the workplace. A movement of God is afoot in the workplace. Henry Blackaby has declared, "I've never seen the activity of God this deeply in the business community as I do right now." Billy Graham has similarly said, "I believe one of the next great moves of God is going to be through the believers in the workplace." After 30 years of watching the spiritual weather vane in the corporate world, we concur. A worldwide spiritual movement is growing in the work place. It didn't start in the church but rather in what the New Testament called the agora, the marketplace. It was in the marketplace where life traveled in the first century, and it's in the agora where life intersects today.

Ministry in and to the business community isn't new. What's new, however, is the adoption of work-life ministry as a core function of the local church. Christian futurist George Barna has predicted that "workplace ministry will be one of the core future innovations in church ministry." A new ministry paradigm is under development. It's a church that makes work-life discipleship and evangelism part of its stated mission and intentional strategy.

The church of the future must adapt a new structure that targets the Monday-through-Friday side of life. The Marketplace Church will focus on where people really traffic, where they really do "salt and light." Its pastors will interact regularly with their congregations during the work week—not just at the hospital bedside, but in the boardroom and on the factory floor.

At the dawn of this realization, many pastors today are making the shift to more effective marketplace ministry. In former days, pastors who preached sermons about work could talk about it only as it related to church committees or service on a church staff. Today pastors are expanding their ministries and messages to be more appropriate to the typical worker out in the world. A paradigm shift is in the works all over the country, even the world. It's a shift from the traditional church program that fostered people's lives at church to a work-life ministry paradigm that fosters their lives at work. Consider the differences between the two mind-sets, as shown on page 123.

The learning curve, however, takes time. Keeping a balanced and integrated life is hard enough without a pastor and church to make the quest harder. Often without even knowing it, a church can cloud the issue—even for churches advanced in their appreciation for the workplace! A few months ago I (John) happened to miss church one weekend. A well-intentioned executive gave a testimony highlighting his commitment to the church. He stated, "The many hours I spend at work are just filler while I bide my time getting to the real meaningful elements of ministry." The five business people who contacted me all voiced the same complaint: "He (the well-intentioned executive) cut our legs right out from under us." Certainly the marketplace sabotage message was unintended—but it happened. Why? Because our ministry framework of what it means to equip, vision, and mobilize believers for the workplace is in the early stages of development.

A SECOND REFORMATION

The Protestant Reformation is widely regarded as one of the most important religious happenings of the second millennium. Johann Gutenberg invented and developed the printing press in the mid-15th century. The mass printing of Bibles enabled something never before possible: mass biblical literacy. The Bible, once hidden in Latin obscurity, was being studied in the vernacular. Information always effects change. The differences between the current state of the church, its teachings, and Scripture became readily apparent.

The Reformation was a significant factor in all of the developments that followed: the progress made in science, medicine, education, theology, the arts, and the development of democracy. These changes became reality largely because of the insatiable interest in Scripture. Thanks to Gutenberg's printing press, the Bible finally became accessible to the common person. The average person could read and understand it; that change became the catalyst for life coming together in ways almost incomprehensible to us today.

Think about it. The Bible became the tool that all people of all nations at all times could hold in their hands and say, "This has connection to my world." People searched for God. Culture—all of humanity—reaped the benefits. When God's truth and life are not confined to a box, big things happen. The world changes beyond human explanation.

Although creativity, innovation, and discovery remain a part of our world, in many arenas, humanity has attempted to put God back in a box. People seem determined to go it alone, to use only human intellect and skill while plumbing the house, selling the toys, managing the project team, operating on the sick, sculpting the statue, or drafting the design for an office building. But when we include God—when we live a "very, very" life—the big becomes bigger, the great becomes greater, the impossible becomes possible.

A second reformation can herald the same dramatic change. Again, we see an insatiable interest in Scripture, but this time with an eye toward its application in our work life, a frontier where biblical influence and spirituality have been seriously lacking. We have a new opportunity to bring God out of the box (as if mortals could keep God there!) and experience God's wonders at work in the marketplace.

It's none too soon, for as British essayist Dorothy Sayers lamented, "In nothing has the church so lost her hold on reality as in her failure to understand and respect the secular vocation, she has allowed work and religion to become separate departments…She has forgotten that the secular vocation is sacred." And if the church no longer sees work as sacred, is it any wonder that so many workers no longer see their faith as sacred? "How can anyone remain interested in a religion," asked Sayers, "that seems to have no concern with nine-tenths of life?"

There are many other workplace residents out there today who have yet to encounter the radical life-changing power of Christ. It's for their sake that we, as individuals and as the body of Christ, must recommit ourselves to a new reformation. It's no longer acceptable to leave on our nightstands the Bibles that were brought to us thanks to Gutenberg. We must walk into the office with the Word written across our work lives. We must integrate our faith and our career.

The church must be restructured to intentionally and systematically nurture these needed changes. Ultimately, there will be no lasting changes to our life at work until there are lasting changes to our church at work.

Whatever we do, we can know this for sure: Our enemy is already active in the marketplace, right here in our town, targeting the work lives of our neighbors with a systematic plan of death and devastation. Like ancient Israel in 1 Samuel, our nation is being ravaged by a Goliath pillaging work lives every day. Will any "Davids" stand in opposition? Who will dare take the stones they have, walk out into the battlefield, and reclaim it in the name of the Lord? Where will we draw the line? If not our places of work, then where? If not in our churches, then where? If not now, when?

This article is adapted by permission of Thomas Nelson Inc., Nashville, from the book *Life@Work: Marketplace Success for People of Faith*, copyright 2005 by John C. Maxwell. All rights reserved. For information on additional Life@Work resources, go to http://www.injoy.com/.

TRADITIONAL CHURCH PARADIGM

The organization of the church is the mission.

Sermons speak in "churchese" about church categories and topics.

Bible stories are told through a ministry lens.

Illustrations are primarily from a pastor's personal world.

Members are pressured to make church a priority over work.

Church health is measured in attendance and buildings.

Everyone is expected to come to the physical location of the church for ministry.

Spiritual formation is focused on church assimilation.

THE COMING WORK-LIFE CHURCH

The daily lives of those in the church is the mission.

Sermons talk in a marketplace-friendly language about being salt and light at work.

Bible characters are painted in all their humanity and daily living.

Illustrations are from the work-a-day world of the audience.

Church structure is simplified to free leaders to fulfill their callings.

Health is measured by the impact of the church's footprint in the community.

The church initiates training, relationships, and programs out into the marketplace.

Spiritual formation includes work-life issues of calling, serving, skill, and character-development.

THE LEADER'S SHADE

by ALAN NELSON | *(September/October 1999)*

My family loves palm trees. Living in Scottsdale, Arizona, allows us to have several in our yard. But one of my favorite trees at our home isn't a palm, nor is it in our yard. It's our neighbor's eucalyptus tree.

Just across our property line to the west stands a huge, 30-foot, leafy giant. The reason I like this tree so much is that in the smoldering Arizona summer, the towering tree blocks the intense sun, providing shade for most of our grassy front lawn in the hottest part of the day. During the heat, shade is invaluable. The tree lets me play ball and tag with my boys in our front yard, when otherwise we'd be cooped up in our air-conditioned house.

Not too long ago, we had to let a wonderful staff member go because it was a ministry mismatch and things weren't working out. As a leader, I took some heat for that decision because people didn't understand the process or principles behind the call. Certainly there was some wear and tear on my emotions. And except for the staff member himself, I was probably pained the most. But sometimes leaders must make the tough calls. You don't always have the opportunity to explain yourself or let your people experience the process.

The responsibility of leadership is to provide shade for your congregation. You're looking out for their long-term welfare, even though there's short-term discomfort. That's why, as a leader, you may sometimes feel lonely in your ministry because of decisions you have to make. But remember, there's always a need for shade.

THE FINE ART OF CHANGE

by CHARLES ARN | *(November/December 1999)*

> *"Thinking like we have is what got us where we are.*
> *It is not going to get us where we are going."*
> —ALBERT EINSTEIN

People, by nature, tend to resist change. Consequently, how you introduce a new idea in your church will greatly affect whether it's eventually adopted. Don't assume that the idea will be naturally accepted on its obvious merits. It won't. In fact, you're much safer—and more likely to be correct—in assuming that the idea will be resisted. Most people are allergic to change.

In a national study on churches' responsiveness to change, Paul Mundey, director of the Andrew Center in Elgin, Illinois, asked pastors what was the most difficult change they'd attempted to make in the church. "Overwhelmingly," he reports, "respondents listed something connected with the worship or the Sunday morning schedule as the most difficult, including:

- *the addition of a worship service, especially a contemporary one;*
- *a change in time for the existing worship service;*
- *a change in time for Sunday school; and*
- *an attempt to introduce more contemporary elements into an existing worship service."*

Here are six guidelines for successfully introducing change, which will be helpful any time a new idea is presented in your church.

1. PRESENT THE IDEA AS A WAY TO REACH AN AGREED-UPON GOAL.

One of the best reasons for a church to spend time developing and adopting a mission statement is to pave the way for change. If there's been previous thought, discussion, and prayer put into a mission statement, and if the congregation has adopted this statement of purpose, then new ideas are more likely to be supported if they're seen as a step toward reaching your church's goals. In the bulletin several years ago, the First Nazarene Church of Pasadena, California included a Q-and-A insert prior to launching a contemporary worship service. The first question read, "Why are two worship service options being studied?" The answer was: "Our Mission Statement states that we intend for ministry to be offered with a diversity of options. This means that any options offered take into consideration the needs of our church family and those of our community. Both experience and research indicate that a seeker-sensitive worship would allow us to have a significant impact on local people who are not now a part of our church fellowship, nor of any other church fellowship."

2. INTRODUCE THE IDEA AS AN ADDITION, NOT A REPLACEMENT.

Most people resist change not for fear of discovering the future, but for fear of discarding the past. If you were to propose a new worship service, for example, members should be assured that the present service won't be changed. The goal is to offer more options so that more people have the opportunity to be a part of the body of Christ. You'll have much more freedom to initiate a new service and try new approaches if those who attend the present service—and enjoy it—aren't asked to give up their service as a result.

3. USHER IN THE IDEA AS A SHORT-TERM EXPERIMENT INSTEAD OF A LONG-TERM COMMITMENT.

Members who question whether the change is an appropriate or wise move for the church will be more open to accepting a trial period in which the new idea is implemented and then evaluated. Agree on a date when the new idea will be reviewed. At that time, collectively evaluate whether or not it's accomplishing its goals. If the experiment is, in fact, a successful step in the pursuit of the church's mission, it'll be far easier at that time to obtain permission for a long-term commitment. If it isn't accomplishing its goals, it's to everyone's advantage to re-evaluate.

Another benefit of an initial short-term trial of the new idea is that we're more tolerant of change if it's seen as a temporary condition. Often we discover that the change isn't as distasteful as we had feared and, in fact, is sometimes more desirable than the past.

"Respondent after respondent shared that the strategy of a 'trial period' made it much easier to introduce change," reports Mundey.

"People knew that the change was not permanent and that there'd be opportunity to evaluate what had been done. That greatly increases the openness of a congregation to experimentation. This strategy also helps those seeking the change because they don't have their necks stuck out so far! If the experiment doesn't work, no one has lost great dignity or reputation because of it."

4. ENCOURAGE ENHANCEMENTS TO CREATE OWNERSHIP.

"Good goals are my goals; bad goals are your goals." If a member feels as if the new idea is something in which he or she has a personal identity, that member will be more likely to support the idea and work for its success. Goal ownership comes through helping to formulate or refine the goal. Ask others for their suggestions on how the new idea can be most effective. In all likelihood their ideas will enhance the result, as well as broaden goal ownership.

5. SOW SEEDS OF CREATIVE DISCONTENT.

Here's a principle of change that applies to all of life, including the church.

"Voluntary change only occurs when there's sufficient discontent with the status quo." For many, the primary comfort of the church is its predictability. Things seem to be the same today as they've been for years. And it's that very stability which causes them to resist change in the church. "The solution," says author Aubrey Malphurs, "is to help those people and their churches discover that everything isn't all right. Point out that to simply continue the present course won't, in all likelihood, realize such a dream."

There's a difference between destructive discontent and constructive discontent. Destructive discontent is a desire to leave the present for a more appealing past. Constructive discontent is a desire to leave the present for a more appealing future.

6. START WITH THE LEADERS.

"A wise leader," observes Doug Murren, "will subscribe to a basic three-step process in presenting new directions to the church:

1) explain the idea to the core group,

2) collaborate with the committed workers, and

3) share with the entire congregation."

As you begin to integrate these six principles of change into your methodology, you'll find that many more of your proposals will be met with positive response, and your church will move forward in creative and effective new ways.

Charles Arn is president of Church Growth, Inc. in Monrovia, California. His book *How to Start a New Service* (Baker) discusses the process of successfully introducing a new style of worship service as a means of outreach to new target groups.

MAKE AT LEAST ONE MISTAKE A WEEK

by RICK WARREN | *(January/February 2005)*

It's not uncommon for me to remind the leaders at Saddleback Church that they have permission to make at least one mistake a week.

I obviously don't want the leaders to fall into sloppy habits, but I do want them to feel free to fail because that means they'll also feel free to take risks! Over the years, I've learned that if I'm not making mistakes, then I'm probably not trying anything new. And if I'm not trying anything new, then I'm not learning; and if I'm not learning, then my leadership will quickly become outdated and perhaps even irrelevant.

Embracing the risk of failure is one of the elements of innovation. So let me encourage you to take risks in your ministry. Don't be afraid to try different methods or to think way, way "out of the box." The great inventor Thomas Edison saw mistakes in a positive light, saying they taught him the things that didn't work, freeing him to discover what would succeed. Edison moved forward from countless mistakes and failures, inventing—among many things—the light bulb.

Nothing great has been accomplished for God without great risk-taking. We need to insist (yes, insist) that all Christ-followers, especially leaders, take risks in their ministry for Christ. Risk-taking ties directly into faith-building. In other words, risk-taking expresses faith in service to God.

No small dreams allowed. One way to teach faithful risk-taking is to take people to Mark 10:27: "...all things are possible with God." Ask your leaders to circle the word *all* and to write the letters *NSD* next to that verse. *NSD* means No Small Dreams. We serve a big God, and God says the size of our faith will determine the size of our blessings in life: "According to your faith will it be done to you" (Matthew 9:29).

A great biblical example of faithful risk-taking is in Matthew 25, where Jesus tells the story of three servants who are given a varying amount of talents by their master just before he goes on a long journey. One servant was given five talents, which he went out and doubled; another servant was given two talents, which he also doubled. When the master returned, he told these servants, "Good work! You did your job well. From now on be my partner" (Matthew 25:23, *The Message*). In most translations, the master describes these servants as faithful. In contrast, the servant who was given one talent proves to be unfaithful, telling his returning master, "...I know you have high standards and hate careless ways, that you demand the best and make no allowances for error. I was afraid I might disappoint you, so I found a good hiding place and secured your money. Here it is, safe and sound down to the last cent" (Matthew 25:24-25, *The Message*).

Jesus says the master was furious, and told the servant, "That's a terrible way to live! It's criminal to live cautiously like that! If you knew I was after the best, why did you do less than the least?

The least you could have done would have been to invest the sum with the bankers, where at least I would have gotten a little interest" (Matthew 25:26-27, *The Message*).

The master then said the single talent should be given to the one who risked the most: "And get rid of this 'play-it-safe' who won't go out on a limb" (Matthew 25:29, *The Message*). The point is—when we're not taking risks with God, we're being unfaithful.

Have you buried your talent? Pastoral leadership is tough. But if we're not taking any risks in ministry, then we're really not exercising faith, and if we're not exercising faith, then we're being faithless. Think about the risks you're taking or that you should be taking in your ministry. For many of us, it means finding a shovel and unearthing the talents that have been hidden for far too long. Once your talent gets dusted off and sees the light of day, you'll be amazed at what God will do with your now-riskable talent, good and faithful servant.

KEEPING CURRENT WITH LEADERS
Asking the Right Questions...

by TAMMY KELLEY | *(March/April 2003)*

How can I stay in touch with my staff and key leaders?

Leaders know the value in mastering the art of asking questions. Great leaders gather information and ideas from other people as they map a course for the future. Good questions provide clarity and focus. Organizations thrive when they create a positive questioning culture and turn away from strict command and control structure.

We have the opportunity to shape staff and volunteer leadership culture and reinforce values simply by asking strategic questions. As people are regularly asked the same questions, they'll start to align their day-to-day activities to achieve the desired answers to the questions.

Here is a form that can be used in several ways, either as a guide for one-on-one conversations or as a format for written reports that people are asked to turn in on a monthly basis.

QUESTIONS REGARDING STATISTICS, DEVELOPMENT, STORIES, AND IDEAS

Complete these questions on a monthly basis to see how staff and volunteer leaders are doing in their areas of ministry. Consider other questions that will help you understand the ethos of each ministry and the ministry leaders.

STATISTICS

1. How many new classes, groups, or teams have been started this month?

2. How many leaders are you responsible for? How many apprentices?

3. Please provide a list of the names of new leaders and apprentices in your ministry.

4. List any groups, classes, or ministry teams that were discontinued.

5. What types of meetings did you have with your leaders? How many were present?

DEVELOPMENT

1. What training events did you do for the people in your ministry area?

2. Did you attend any training or continuing education events?

3. What books, magazines, or Web sites have you read? Any new insights?

4. Any potential new staff or leaders that you see on the horizon?

5. Any particular concern that you have or an area where you need personal support?

6. Are you growing spiritually?

7. Are you having fun in your ministry work?

STORIES

1. Any first-time commitments to Jesus in your ministry area?

2. Who are you mentoring? How are you mentoring them?

3. Any great stories of people's lives being changed in your ministry?

4. Any great stories of people in your ministry making an impact on the lives of others?

IDEAS

1. Any comments or ideas that you would like to share?

2. Any ideas that you've seen or heard somewhere else that could be transferred to your ministry?

CLEAN UP CULTURAL CHALLENGES

"[The church's] responsibility is not only to hold to the basic, scriptural principles of the Christian faith, but to communicate these unchanging truths 'into' the generation in which it is living. Every generation has the problem of learning how to speak meaningfully to its own age. It cannot be solved without an understanding of the changing existential situation which it faces."

—FRANCES SCHAEFFER

(November/December 2004, pg. 79)

DOROTHY LEADERSHIP

by BRIAN MCCLAREN | *(November/December 2000)*

Okay, I admit it. I spent most of the '80s and early '90s wishing I could be just like Bill Hybels, Rick Warren, or John Maxwell. They were successful. They appeared unflinchingly confident. They were powerful, knowledgeable, and larger than life. I'd go to their seminars and return home feeling wildly inspired and mildly depressed. How could I feel those two things at the same time? If you've attended their seminars, you probably don't need me to explain.

But if you do need me to explain, think back to the biblical story of David, when he tried to wear Saul's armor for his battle with Goliath. Imagine that he actually wore armor that was XXL when he was a regular M (or even S) guy. He would've come back looking like a partially opened—and partially eaten—can of sardines.

I realize I wasn't the only one who thought that the best image of the successful pastor was the CEO, the alpha male, the armored knight, or the corporate hero. Thousands of us tried on that armor, and the results—in our churches and in our personal lives—weren't pretty. Of course, the suit fit some of us (for example, I think that Hybels, Warren, and Maxwell really are XXLs), but most of us eventually realized that if we were going to be of any use to God, we'd better be ourselves. What a novel idea!

About the time I was reaching that conclusion, I was going through my "postmodern conversion." I was seeing the pattern or matrix of modernity giving way to a new pattern, and I was beginning to see how my whole understanding of Christianity fit snugly within the modern matrix. I wondered how ministry, theology, spirituality, and evangelism would change as the matrix changed. And I wondered how leadership would change, too.

Somewhere in the middle of these musings, a strange memory returned—the scene in *The Wizard of Oz* when little Toto pulls back the curtain to reveal that the great wizard of Oz is a rather normal guy hiding behind an imposing image. It struck me that the 1940s world that produced the film was in many ways a world at the height of modernity, a world enamored with Superman, the Lone Ranger, and other great men. It also struck me that by exposing the wizard as a fraud, the film was probing an unexpressed cultural doubt, giving voice to a rising misgiving, displaying an early pang of discontent with its dominant model of larger-than-life leadership. And it made me wonder what image of leadership would replace the great wizard.

The answer, of course, appeared in the next scene. No, it wasn't the lion, the scarecrow, or the tin man. It was Dorothy.

At first glance Dorothy is all wrong as a model of leadership for that era. She was the wrong gender (female) and the wrong age (young). Rather than being a person with all the answers, who knows what's up, where to go, and what's what, she's lost, a seeker, often bewildered, and vulnerable. These characteristics would disqualify her from modern leadership. But they serve as her best credentials for postmodern leadership.

In the world of Christian ministry, we can identify 10 wizardly characteristics of modern leadership. (You'll notice the masculine pronoun used exclusively here.)

Bible analyst: The modern Christian leader dissects the Bible like a scientist dissects a fetal pig, to gain knowledge through analysis. And in modernity, knowledge is power.

Broadcaster: Somehow when one amplifies his voice electronically and adds a little reverb, his power quotient goes up in modernity. Being slick, being smooth, being big, being "on the air"—that's what makes you a leader.

Objective technician: The organization—church or ministry—is a machine, and the leader knows how to work the machine, how to make it run, how to tweak it, and how to engineer (or re-engineer) it. It's the object, and he's the subject.

Warrior/salesman: Modern leadership is about conquest—"winning" souls, launching "crusades," "taking" this city (country, whatever) for Jesus. And it's about marketing, getting, buying, and selling (and sometimes selling out).

Careerist: The modern leader earns credentials, grasps the bottom rung of the ladder, and climbs, climbs, climbs—whether he's a stock boy who would be CEO or a young preacher on the rise.

Problem-solver: Come to him, and he'll fix you.

Apologist: Come to him, and he'll tell you why he's right and your doubt or skepticism is wrong.

Threat: One of the most powerful and underrated weapons of the modern Christian leader has been the threat of exclusion. The sword is normally kept in its sheath, but through mocking caricatures and other forms of rhetorical demonization, a gifted orator can make you fear that if you don't agree with/follow/submit to his leadership, you'll be banished—like the wizard bellowing threats from behind his curtain.

Knower: The modern Christian leader is—or appears—supremely confident in his opinions, perspectives, beliefs, systems, and formulations. While the rest of us question and doubt, he's the answer man who knows.

Solo act: There's only room for one in the wizard's control booth, and there's only room for one at the top of the church organizational chart.

When you think of Dorothy, the picture's extremely different. Instead of sitting pretty in a control booth, she's stuck in a predicament—still a little dizzy from the tornado, lost, far from home, and needing to find the way. As she sets out on her journey, she finds other needy people (not people exactly, but you get the point). One in need of courage, another in need of intelligence, and another in need of a heart. She believes that their varying needs can be fulfilled on a common quest, and her earnestness, her compassion, her determination, and her youthful spunk galvanize them into a foursome—five, with Toto—singing and traveling down the yellow brick road—together. Dorothy doesn't have the knowledge to help them avoid all problems and dangers; she doesn't protect them from all threats and temptations. But she doesn't give up, and her passion holds strong. And in the end, they all get what they need.

Maybe one of the film's many enduring delights is hidden in Dorothy's unwizardly leadership charisma. Maybe people in the 1940s were just beginning to yearn for a way of leadership that now is becoming ascendant—a post-wizard, postmodern kind of leadership. (And you'll notice pronouns for both genders here.)

Spiritual sage instead of Bible analyst: As we move beyond modernity, we lose our infatuation with analysis, knowledge, information, facts, and belief systems—and those who traffic in them. Instead, we're attracted to leaders who possess that elusive quality of wisdom (think of James 3:13), who practice spiritual disciplines, and whose lives are characterized by depth of spiritual practice (not just by tightness of belief system). These leaders possess a moral authority more closely linked to character than intellectual credentials; they're more sages than technicians. It's their slow, thoughtful, considered answer that convinces, not the snap-your-fingers-I-know-that-kind-of-answer-man-know-it-all-ness. Dorothy has this "softer" authority, a reflection of her earnestness and kindness as much as her intellectual acumen.

Listener instead of broadcaster: In the postmodern world, it's not how loudly you shout; it's how deeply you listen that counts. Just as Dorothy engages her traveling companions by listening to their stories and evoking their needs, the postmodern leader creates a safe place that attracts a team, and then she empowers them with the amazing power of a listening heart.

Spiritual friend instead of objective technician: Think of the difference between a scientist objectively studying chimpanzees and a crusader dedicated to saving them from extinction. In modernity a leader loves his organization and loves his ambition, his strategic plan, his goals; but on this side of the transition, leaders love their teams, and those to whom their teams are sent. Or more perversely put—in modernity, 1 Corinthians 13 would read, "If I have all love and would lay down my life for my friends, but have not knowledge, I am a wispy wimp and a poor excuse for a leader." Beyond modernity we return to Paul's original meaning.

Dancer instead of warrior/salesman: In a world plagued by ethnic hatred and telemarketers, every voice adding stridency and sales pressure to the world is one voice too many. Nobody wants to be "won to Christ" or "taken for Jesus" in one of our "crusades," nor do they want to be subjected to a sales pitch for heaven that sounds for all the world like an invitation to check out a time-share vacation resort. A presentation of the gospel that sounds like a military ultimatum or like a slick sales pitch will dishonor the gospel for postmodern people. Instead think of leadership—and especially evangelism—as a dance. You hear the music that I don't hear, and you know how to move to its rhythm. Gently you help me begin to hear its music, feel its rhythm, and learn to move to it with grace and joy. A very different kind of leadership, don't you agree?

Amateur instead of careerist: The root of the word *amateur* is "amar"—to love. Most of us in Christian leadership know that seeing ministry as a career can quickly quench the motivation of love. How can we keep that higher motivation alive? How can Christian leadership be for us less like the drudgery of a job and more like the joy of a day golfing, fishing, playing soccer, or whatever…not something we have to do, but something we get to do? The professionalization of ministry will be one of the harmful legacies of modernity, I believe.

Quest creator instead of problem-solver: The man at the top of modern leadership is the guy you go to for answers and solutions. No doubt there are times when that's what we need now, too. But postmodern leaders will be as interested in creating new problems, in setting new challenges, in launching new adventures…as in solving, finishing, or facilitating old ones. Dorothy does this: She helps her companions trade their old problems (birds landing on the scarecrow, the tin man being paralyzed by rust, the lion faking bravado) for a new quest. Of course this is what Jesus does, too. He doesn't solve the problems of the Pharisees. (How can we get these stupid crowds to know and obey the law as we do?) He creates new ones. (Seek first the kingdom of God.)

Apologizer instead of apologist: Instead of defending old answers, the new kind of leader will often apologize for how inadequate he is. In modernity you gained credibility by always being right; in postmodernity you gain authority by admitting when you're wrong (think of the Pope's visit to the Middle East in early 2000) and apologizing humbly. That kind of humility, that vulnerability, was one of Dorothy's most winsome—and leaderlike—characteristics.

Includer instead of threat: The only threat Dorothy poses is the threat of inclusion, not exclusion. She basically threatens you with acceptance; you're part of her journey, a member of her team, unless you refuse and walk away. That kind of leadership strikes me as gospel leadership, and it reminds me of someone else—Jesus.

Seeker instead of knower: Oddly, Dorothy's appeal as a leader arises from being lost and being passionate about seeking a way home. Does it ever strike you as odd in contemporary Christian jargon that it's the pre-Christians who are called seekers? Where does that leave the Christians? Shouldn't the Christian leader be the lead seeker?

Team-builder instead of solo act: All along her journey, Dorothy welcomed company. She was glad for a team. By the end of their journey, the lion, the scarecrow, and the tin man have joined Dorothy as peers, partners, and friends. Her style of leadership was empowering and ennobling, not patronizing, paternalistic, and dependency-creating. So effective was her empowering of them that they were able to say a tearful goodbye and move on to their own adventures.

I know, you're thinking, *Why take a silly movie so seriously?* You're right—it's just a movie. But I find the film's repudiation of more traditional modern leadership to be fascinating, maybe an early expression of a cultural shift that we're more fully experiencing today.

And ultimately, of course, I find in Dorothy's way of leadership many echoes of our Lord's leadership teachings. After all, you can never imagine the great Oz washing his subjects' feet or booming out, "I no longer call you servants, but friends."

Maybe some of us are trying hard to be something we're not. Maybe we're imitating styles of leadership that are becoming outdated and inappropriate. That's not to say we don't have a lot to learn, but maybe the best thing that could happen to us would be to have the curtain pulled back to reveal us not as XXL superheroes, but regular size M men and women. Maybe then, with the amplifiers turned off and the images dropped, we'll hear Jesus inviting us to learn new ways of leading for his cause.

LEADERSHIP LESSONS
FROM ANTARCTICA

by THOM SCHULTZ | *(July/August 2005)*

Thousands of penguins huddled on the ice-covered ground like a
tuxedoed audience for a world premier. They watched and waddled
as their swimming brethren performed a water pageant—leaping
out of the sea like frenetic little porpoises.

Why do they rocket out of the water? Our expedition leader listed several possible reasons. Among them: Penguins are prey to predators such as the swift-moving leopard seal. Penguins must be wily enough to capture their fish for sustenance and clever enough to elude the wicked jaws of the predators.

The attentive audience on shore began moving toward the frigid water. One by one they followed their apparent leader across the slippery surface. This leader paused at the water's edge and glanced about—perhaps weighing the thoughts of a tasty lunch with the dangers that lurk below the waves. He looked at his followers once again and plunged into the Weddell Sea. The others splashed in right behind him.

I watched for hours last December as these whimsical birds taught unexpected lessons on organizational leadership. Maybe it was the numbing effects of sitting motionless on a slab of blue ice. But I began envisioning these creatures as well-dressed church staffers, lay leaders, and volunteers. While some bickered over who had the rights to nesting pebbles, others sledded down snowy slopes on their bellies— oblivious to everyone else around them. And others seemed more mission-minded, determined to get to the day's work: fishing.

In addition to my addiction to adventure travel, organizational culture and leadership fascinate me. I'm blessed to lead a professional staff of 300 at our Group Publishing headquarters. And my work affords me the opportunity to study and consult with churches of all sizes. Over the past 30 years I've seen many different approaches to organizational leadership. Some have worked. Others have bred terribly dysfunctional work environments. But one thing is clear: Leaders shape the culture of an organization—for better or worse.

Our organization has been named a "best workplace" in regional and national studies. People sometimes ask, "What's your secret?" I've thought about that a lot. I've come to the conclusion that the answer is really quite simple: Remember your mission, and treat your staff as friends. That means prioritizing what's most important, which should reflect your mission. And it means wanting the best for one another, serving one another, wanting one another to grow and succeed.

Pursuing this formula for organizational and ministry success requires a particular style of leadership. I've seen other styles tried,

but they often fail. I call the ones that don't work "The Boss" and "The Protector." The style that works is simply called "The Leader." Let's take a look at each of these.

THE BOSS

When you think of The Boss, what images come to your mind? Old-time authoritarian mayors such as Chicago's Richard J. Daley? the vicious supervisor you had in a dead-end job? a military basic training instructor? Bruce Springsteen? (Just kidding.)

Bosses rely on authority and hierarchy. Bosses enjoy giving orders. And they usually don't mind receiving orders from their superiors. This leadership style works for some people in some settings. In fact, The Boss is necessary in many organizations, such as the military, police and fire departments, and prisons.

It's a red flag for me when I hear leader-wannabes say (in various ways) that their goal is to acquire authority over others. The Boss relishes the control over other people. That desire can be toxic in the church.

And The Boss wouldn't work well in a penguin colony. That'd be like putting the leopard seal in charge. Sure, you might be able to scare the penguins into compliance, but they'd never develop into their full potential.

THE PROTECTOR

What images come to mind when you think of a protective person? I think of an overly protective parent of a 9-year-old child.

One day the child comes home from school crying that the teacher is mean and made the child sit in the corner. Immediately the protective parent zooms off to the school in the minivan, storms into the principal's office, and demands the firing of the teacher.

In the world of leadership, The Protector's top priority is to make sure the staff member's feelings aren't hurt. The Protector wants to insulate the person at all costs from any discomfort.

As with The Boss, The Protector isn't always bad. We need "protectors" in society to look out for the safety and well-being of children, the elderly, and others without the ability or power to protect themselves. In the penguin colony, I observed many good penguin parents protecting their young hatchlings from swooping, hungry raptors. But as the young mature, they don't need parents to sit on them but to release them to become fully functioning penguins.

In the context of ministry leadership, Protectors tend to sit on people in ways that may appear to be kind and loving. But they're stunting the growth of their followers—and inhibiting the growth of the community.

THE LEADER

In an effective ministry, The Leader focuses on the mission of Christ as manifested in the organization's goals and objectives. The Leader develops fully functional staff members who are capable of doing big things to fulfill the mission.

The Leader's first priority is the success of the organization's mission. Then The Leader cares tremendously about the staff and helps them be successful in furthering the organization's mission.

That's like my penguin friend that led a waddling parade of cohorts from the safety of the nest to the water's edge. Somehow he got everyone headed in the same direction, assessed the risk of the hunt, and led the first plunge.

THE "GO BUTTONS" OF EACH TYPE

Each of the three leadership styles has a dominant "go button"—the interior force that drives their behavior. The go button for The Boss is a thirst for personal power. If the team benefits, fine. But if given the choice, The Boss would rather control others with mediocre mission results than be under someone else's leadership with greater mission results.

The Protector's go button is a little harder to pinpoint for the unwary. Protectors appear to be kind, loving, and concerned for their staff. But after you strip back all the layers, Protectors crave the love of their followers. Protectors believe that if they can simply protect their people from all harm, the followers will love their Protectors. Protectors are ready to sacrifice the organization's mission in order to avoid hurting any team member's feelings.

What about The Leader's go button? The Leader's primary go

button is the success of the mission. Leaders support not only the mission, but also each other so that the mission succeeds.

THEOLOGICAL MOORINGS OF THE LEADER

What clues can we find in God's nature that point us to a leadership style that works in ministry?

The Boss excludes people's sense of choice and development. Everything is decided for them. That doesn't describe God's design for us. God gives us choice.

The Protector wants to protect everyone from any possible discomfort. However, God didn't designate comfort as the ultimate goal. To the contrary, God allowed the ultimate discomfort when he sent his Son as a sacrifice to die for us.

Jesus' mission was the ultimate goal. He demonstrated his devotion to the mission from the start. It was his first priority. And he invested purposefully in his followers to help them be successful in furthering the mission. And in the process, he called them not servants, but friends (John 15:15).

WHAT ABOUT YOUR LEADERSHIP?

In leadership training, I walk leaders through 10 common situations that Christian leaders often face. These scenarios demonstrate the difference in how Bosses, Protectors, and Leaders deal with different typical situations. I have outlined them on pages 164-165. I encourage you to walk through those 10 situations with your staff and volunteers. Let's look at the first three here to get you going.

SITUATION #1: STAFFER COMES TO YOU WITH A QUESTION OR PROBLEM

Look at the first situation on page 164. A staffer comes to you with a question or a problem on his or her mind. The Boss tells the staffer what to do. Remember, The Boss gives and takes orders. The Protector essentially tells the staffer, "Well, I'll do it for you and thereby guard you from any discomfort."

In contrast to The Boss and The Protector, The Leader listens to the staffer and then asks, "Well, what would you do?" It's very likely that The Leader knows what to do in the situation and knows it would be expedient to tell the staffer what to do. However, The Leader's objective is to develop people to be wildly successful within the mission of the organization. Leaders develop new leaders. Leaders stretch their staff, rather than giving them all the answers. In time, the developing staffer will learn to bring solutions instead of problems.

I admit that this one is hard for me. When staffers come to me with a question or problem that I have been through a thousand times, it's all I can do to bite my tongue and not give them the answer. My "boss" starts to come out, and I just want to get on with things. I'm thinking about all the things I've got to do, and it's more expedient for me to tell them the answer. I have to use a lot of discipline to slow down, edit myself, and allow them to struggle a little bit to develop their own solutions.

SITUATION #2: STAFFER HAS A COMPLAINT ABOUT ANOTHER STAFFER

The staffer comes to you with a complaint about another staffer or volunteer. (I'm sure that never happens in your church, right?) The Boss orders the staffer to "get back to work." The Boss doesn't want to deal with "touchy, feely" stuff. In contrast, The Protector goes to battle the "offending party" on behalf of the staffer. The Protector appears to want peace and harmony, but the real goal of The Protector is to be loved by the staffer and to quell discomfort.

The Leader helps the staffer brainstorm appropriate responses and solutions to the problem, and then urges the staffer to handle it. The Leader asks the staffer to report back how the situation was resolved. The Leader views people as fully functioning adults and sees them as capable to learn how to handle situations in a functional way.

SITUATION #3: A KEY LEADERSHIP DECISION NEEDS TO BE MADE

Let's look at the third example. A key leadership decision needs to be made. It might be the selection of volunteers for a ministry. As the director of that ministry, it's your responsibility to make the decision. The Boss simply decides without any outside input. The Protector may "hold elections" or wait for a 100 percent agreement with the decision. Often the key decision is never really made—out of fear of discomfort or the loss of love from the protected.

The Leader listens intently to staff input and values others' good ideas, but also knows that it's his or her responsibility to make the important decision. The Leader makes the best possible decision so that the organization's mission is advanced, and then invests significant energy in helping others to succeed with the decision.

TAKE THE PLUNGE

In between watching penguins flying in and out the water, sailing through ancient mountains of azure blue ice, and wandering through the vast open spaces, I had a chance to reflect on God's creation, his order, his desires for his people, and his mission.

Some of the ice around me was 2,000 years old. It was here when Jesus walked the earth. The ice was here when he called out his early followers—ordinary fishermen. It was here when he led them to cast their nets for a spectacular catch.

Perched on this ancient ice I watched the older penguins demonstrate their astute fishing prowess to the younger ones. Among the inherent dangers they led another generation to know and follow the mission of becoming master catchers of fish.

So too has our Master modeled how to be master catchers of followers for him.

WHAT'S YOUR LEADERSHIP STYLE?

Leadership Challenges	What the Boss Does	What the Protector Does	What the Leader Does
1. Staffer has a question or problem.	Tells staffer what to do.	Tells staffer, "I'll do it for you."	Asks staffer, "What would you do?"
2. Staffer comes with a complaint about another staffer.	Orders staffer to get back to work.	Goes to "offending" person and advocates on staffer's behalf.	Helps brainstrom responses staffer may use. Urges staffer to go directly to the other person.
3. A key leadership decision needs to be made.	Decides without staff input and hands out marching orders.	Holds elections or waits for consensus among all staff.	Listens to staff input but makes independent decision.
4. Church wants to add a new ministry or project.	Orders staff to get it done.	Resists or refuses ministry or project because it's "too hard" on staff.	Assesses resources and proposes plan and budget for getting the work done.
5. Staffer asks for greater responsibility for which he or she isn't ready.	Tells staffer to concentrate on present job; appoints somebody else.	Grants the added responsibility even if there's a high probability the staffer isn't ready for it.	Helps staffer discover qualifications necessary for advancement— and how staffer might acquire qualifications. Appoints somebody else.

Leadership Challenges	What the Boss Does	What the Protector Does	What the Leader Does
6. Staffer struggles with a decision.	Lets staffer struggle alone. Punishes staffer if poor decision is made.	Makes decision for staffer.	Helps staffer weigh pros and cons then lets staffer decide.
7. Approach to teamwork.	Strives to make self look good.	Strives to make people in his or her area feel good.	Strives to do what's best for the whole ministry and staff.
8. Circulation of negative talk about other leaders in the congregation.	Stays silent. Ignores staffer's negative comments.	Utters negative comments about other leaders.	Openly supports other leaders, giving benefit of the doubt and stresses need for open and positive talk.
9. Communication of ministry vision and direction.	"Here's what I want you to do."	"Here's what the pastor (or other leader) wants so I guess we have to do it."	"Here's where we're all going. Let's get on board!"
10. Empowerment of staff to take more responsibility.	Delegates, abdicates, and moves on. Blames staff if things go awry.	Protects individuals from assuming "too much" responsibility or making significant decisions independently.	Trains staff, delegates the responsibility and decisions, coaches staff, stays informed about staff decisions, and provides feedback to staff.

FROM GLADIATOR TO IRRITATOR

by RON MARTOIA | *(November/December 2003)*

The hero model of leadership has fallen on hard times. I thoroughly enjoyed watching *Gladiator*, and for lessons on leadership, there may be some good clips to extract. But gladiator grunts and brawn won't work very well in my church setting; I just don't think people will get it. I think they might conclude I have some ego issues; and to be honest, I'm not sure about the costume. I do admit, however, showing up to a board meeting with some of those weapons may at times be helpful...hmmm.

In their volume *Organizing Genius* (Perseus Books), Bennis and Biederman announce the demise of The Great Man (Woman) model of leadership. They adeptly concluded in their book, "None of us is as smart as all of us." Not particularly revolutionary as insights go, but this finding seems more widespread and widely owned than ever. An era of leadership seems to be closing.

The point leader as CEO has been found bankrupt, and not

just in small contexts. The leader as CEO is even worn out and tired in the billion-dollar, multinational marketplace. Command and control are out, connect and collaborate are in. Talk of teaming, facilitating, fostering, and generating abound in the high-end business sections of the bookstores and in the finest business schools in the land. This is a good shift for me as well. I've always hated the command-and-control business suits and secretly wondered what ding-a-ling suggested tying a 2.5-inch-wide piece of silk around your neck to create an air of sophistication, especially when coupled with a starched, stiff-as-a-board white oxford. My best guess is this was an early fashion conspiracy by a couple of irate spouses who figured they could use that Italian silk as a noose if push came to shove.

The fact is, times are changing and "times" are the things that mold leaders. A closing of an era implies the transition to a new one. What implications does this have for the leadership enterprise and our leadership lexicon?

The world acknowledges there's a shift underway, and we'd be well-served to observe the changes as well. And these aren't just any changes; these are changes at the level of mental models.

MENTAL MODELS

Mental models are the deeply held beliefs we have about how the world works and the way it should be. Mental models are similar to assumptions but can be much more complex and detailed. When the world changes and our mental models don't, we're headed for obsolescence.

Children want to be treated in age-appropriate ways. Our mindsets—our mental models—have to adapt as our children grow, or their growth becomes stunted and their development truncated.

I contend that our leadership needs a full overhaul in the mental model department. One of the universal changes that has occurred in leadership is the movement from "either/or" to one that is "both/and."

Mental models—due to their invisibility—are often hard to uncover and identify. Most of the time they're tacit, not explicit. I can think of at least four mental models I see a need to shift as we lead our communities into this new world.

Rev. Thought: As you read about the four mental models and shifts, pull out some paper, grab your favorite pen, and create your own checklist regarding what changes need to occur in your leadership style.

1. Leadership is about finding the answers we need. Few of us would disagree that this is the way many people view us—a spiritual and biblical treasure-trove for any and every question imagined. This is what drives most phone calls to your office and why most people want to meet with you. You're the answer person.

Obviously, this is a vestige of our modern world where knowledge is considered weapon #1, and the one with the most knowledge wins. I'm not saying knowledge is unimportant or even peripheral. But I think I have too easily adopted the role that leadership is essentially about helping people find their answers, and as the point leader, I'm to find our organizational answers.

Rev. Thought: Do you find yourself always ready to give an answer? When do you do it most—in your preaching, teaching, counseling, or elsewhere? Take Jesus' example to heart. Intentionally begin asking questions in response to questions posed to you. Also, do you have someone you can trust to ask you the hard questions? If not, look around and ask God to prompt you and direct you toward that person(s) who can challenge you. Write down their name and when you plan on contacting them.

Shift: Leadership is more about the right questions being asked in the right context at the right time. Jesus' life and ministry were full of answering questions with questions. In the Gospel of Mark there are more than 60 episodes where there's conversation with Jesus. In those episodes, Jesus asks no fewer than 50 questions. If we're to take any cue from Jesus at all, we need to become premier provocateurs and allow the organic byproducts of team ownership and community consensus to naturally flow.

Our leadership post is more agitant and irritant than encyclopedic. We might say we must shift our leadership from "gladiator" to "irritator and agitator." The right questions in the right place at the right time are irritating and they systemically agitate. I have some people in my life who ask well-placed questions. Why do you feel that way, Ron? What is the root of that, Ron? What do you think that should tell you about how you communicate, Ron? I don't mind telling you, this is irritating as all get-out! But I've become convinced this may be leadership at its absolute finest.

2. Leadership is about skill set acquisition. Most of us are obsessed with skill learning, as we probably should be, but allow me to point out that the New Testament isn't real big on skill set development as much as who we're becoming.

When you think about Jesus' training window, it was remarkably brief. Think about the average pew-sitter in the church and the number of sermons, talks, Bible studies, and small groups they have endured, yea, even survived. And yet many of them will tell you they're unable to lead anything because they don't yet have the skills; they feel unequipped.

Compare this to Jesus' training-time horizon. How long were

the disciples in training before Jesus sent them out on their first weekend of speaking in various villages? Of course, we don't have a clear answer. But this we do know: Jesus was only with the disciples from start to finish for three years. It's more than possible the disciples only had a number of months of training before they were asked to speak to entire villages.

Jesus was more concerned about their character than their skill. Being precedes doing; it isn't the other way around.

Shift: Leadership is more about fully being, inhabiting my destiny, and having an inner morphic dynamic with God. Skill set acquisition is only helpful when you're in relationship with God. It's relatively clear from the research of guys such as Robert Clinton in his book, *Strategic Concepts That Clarify a Focused Life: A Self-Study Manual Defining*

Rev. Thought: Do you find yourself spending more and more time learning and reading about particular skill sets that will help your church or ministry grow? When's the last time you intentionally spent a large part of your schedule or created consistent space within your calendar to cultivate your personal relationship with God? Remember, leadership leaks. And your personal relationship with God—or lack thereof—will be reflected in the leaders you're spending time with in ministry. You might even want to ask them what kind of leadership you're leaking. The answers may surprise you.

and Applying Focused Life Concepts to Leaders Today (Barnabas Publishers), that the more we understand about our gifts, passions, and relationship with God, the more we see our leadership emerge with spiritual authority.

Who I am creates a certain kind of feel and ethos in which people either thrive or attempt to survive. The ethos created is more important to transforming a life than learning a particular skill. Skill without the ethos will lead to mechanical execution. Ethos, providing a greenhouse for growth, will lead to organic connection with a byproduct of new skills adopted.

When I work to keep my life sharp before God, my creativity soaring, my sensitivity delicate, the ethos that results will engender the same thing in my team. Skill set acquisition happens in those greenhouses much more through osmosis and coaching on the fly than through a class taken or a training session attended.

3. Leadership is about arriving at some out-there goal, taking a summit, or storming a hill. For so long we've heard that leadership is about visioning, motivating, and inspiring people toward an end that enables them to enter into something bigger than themselves. Of course, that's part of leadership. But Jesus seemed to attend more to the feel of his community than to the strategic plans or objectives for that community. It's hard to escape the Sermon on the Mount being more about creating certain community feel through character development than some big out-there goal Jesus was trying to propel them toward.

Rev. Thought: Unfortunately, part of the "taking the hill" in our ministries is duplicating what someone else has done in their ministry. The "model" is often more important than identifying and cultivating who we are within our cultural and community setting. How can you love God and love others within your current culture, and how are you translating that to your leaders, congregation, and community? Write it down.

Shift: Leadership is more about crafting the present ethos, which is the organic soil of the emerging ministry tomorrow. Throughout the New Testament, Jesus is hanging out with his disciples. The shape and flavor of that hanging out is fairly detailed; there were seaside fish fries, village-to-village hikes, ministry debriefing and results discussions, coaching through disappointments, and preparation for emerging realities.

Does this mean the "Where are we headed?" question is irrelevant? Hardly. Where we're headed, however, is a secondary question. Without the ethos and environment by which a team can experience deep life and community together, the experience of summit scaling is rather dissatisfying.

My team loves grandiose dreaming. And we do our fair share. But Jesus made clear the whole enchilada can be stated in two simple phrases—love God and love each other. Our job is to make sure that kind of life is flowing in and around our teams. When it flows, momentum kicks in, and momentum rightly directed creates velocity toward the summit.

4. Leadership is about serial sequencing. Serial sequencing is about making sure everyone is thoroughly trained before they're cut loose to invest in others. There's a proper serial sequence that must be followed to make sure people are really "qualified" before they do anything. This is a deeply embedded mental model.

> *Rev. Thought:* OK, we know this is messy, but isn't most of life messy? Find the balance for your ministry in regard to how much pre-service training is necessary and for what areas of service. The sooner people begin serving, the sooner they experience God's presence and guidance in their lives. It's a journey, so help them enjoy their journey, giving and receiving simultaneously.

We put people through a whole bunch of training and then—and only then—do we deem them prepared to invest in someone else's life.

A probing question, though, is how much training did the disciples have before they were sent out into the villages to preach their first messages?

Shift: Leadership is about parallel simultaneity. The Jesus model of training was "on the job." The total time Jesus had with the disciples was three years. Quite obviously, they were sent to begin their public preaching ministry much earlier than the three-year mark. Jesus clearly thought the best model of training was the nexus of mountainside retreat, where there were talking-head segments (hence the Sermon on the Mount in Matthew 5–7) with praxis elements where they debriefed their observations of Jesus' ministry and their own. They were training and being trained simultaneously.

Isn't this the way life really is? We're constantly learning and, hopefully, constantly pouring our lives into someone else. There's no set of competencies that enable us to say we've now arrived and are ready to train someone else. Of course, there are some baseline minimums, but I secretly think our minimums are far more elaborate, complex, and detailed than the minimums Jesus held to.

These are at least four of the mental models that need to shift for the new era we're living in. As you've taken the time to read, digest, apply, and take action steps regarding these four models, perhaps you've identified others that you're experiencing. Do the same with each of those, questioning them and identifying shifts that need to occur.

UNDERSTANDING THE SHIFTS IN LEADERSHIP

Looking for a good read that will help you navigate the changes in mental models of leadership? Check out any or all of these resources.

Organizing Genius: The Secrets of Creative Collaboration (Perseus Books Group) by Patricia Ward Biederman and Warren G. Bennis

Strategic Concepts That Clarify a Focused Life: A Self-Study Manual Defining and Applying Focused Life Concepts to Leaders Today (Barnabas Publishers) by Robert Clinton

Jesus Asked (Zondervan) by Conrad Gempf

Interactive Excellence: Defining and Developing New Standards for the Twenty-First Century (Ballantine Books) by Edwin Schlossberg

Morph! The Texture of Leadership for Tomorrow's Church (Group Publishing, Inc.) by Ron Martoia

The Dance of Change: The Challenges to Sustaining Momentum in Learning Organizations (Doubleday) by Peter Senge, et al.

Deep Change: Discovering the Leader Within (Jossey-Bass) by Robert E. Quinn

Working Beneath the Surface: Attending to the Soul's "Hidden Agenda" for Wholeness, Fulfillment, and Deep Spiritual Healing (Executive Excellence) by Thomas Riskas

LOW-FAT LEADERSHIP

Discover Five Leadership Nutrients That
Provide Health and Vitality for Your Ministry

by DAVE FLEMING | *(September/October 2002)*

The writer of Ecclesiastes wrote, "To the making of many books there is no end." With prophetic tone, these words could easily describe the

current proliferation of published material on the topic of leadership. Leadership has become one of the most written about topics on the market today. It's a feast that came out of famine.

You'd think that all this emphasis on leadership would be a good thing. Well, it is…sort of. The glut of ideas, thoughts, writings, and programs currently available makes it difficult to find the important hidden in the excess. Can you say bloated? This is the condition of leaders who flit from one leadership theory to another just because it's new. Of course, the reverse happens just as often. Can you say starving? This is the condition of so many other leaders.

They shrug their shoulders at the "latest and greatest" and settle for "tried and true" theories and practices that have served them—so they think—for many years.

Here's the deal: When it comes to leadership, stuffing (running after the latest and greatest) or starving (sticking with the shrinking familiar) leads to the same basic problem—a lack of good "leader nutrition." The ironic situation of the day is that with the largest menu of leadership food ever assembled, many leaders are still basically spiri-

tually malnourished or overweight. This is due primarily to the fact that leaders haven't yet learned how to find, store, retrieve, and use the ideas, thoughts, and practices that are truly nutritious. In other words, they lack the staples of good leader nutrition that would provide a baseline of health and vitality.

A leadership "diet" low in fat and high in nutrition will not only provide you with health, but also with a place—or system—to store all of the ideas you discover in your interaction with leadership material and other leaders. The five leader nutrients create a system and a storage place for the practices and ideas you discover today so that you have them for tomorrow.

> When asked to identify their primary spiritual gifts, this is what senior pastors said...
> 40% said preaching or teaching
> 12% said pastoring
> 6% mentioned encouragement
> 4 % said leadership
> www.barna.org

NUTRIENT ONE: JOURNEY

"Life is in the journey, not the destination."

"We never arrive, but are always arriving."

"Enjoy the journey."

We've probably all heard these tired but true phrases and understand their importance. Since these words are so familiar and so important, why do they keep slipping out of our lives like a bar of soap on a bad shower day? Humans, and especially leaders, have a tendency to reduce the journey to an incident or a routine void of adventure. Kevin Cashman, in his book, *Leadership From the Inside Out* (Executive Excellence) reminds us, "We tend to view leadership as an external event. We see it only as something people do...Leadership is not simply something we do. It comes from somewhere inside us. Leadership is a process, an intimate expression of who we are. It is our being in action."

Life is a journey. We initiate leadership when we seek to actualize this truth (supported and enabled by God's grace) in our personal lives. Personal leadership begins when we realize that life emerges moment by moment and that we can learn to discover and discern this emergence. As we do this, we connect with our always-unfolding destiny—our being in action. Adventures don't come with trip ticks—especially the adventure of life. We must live our way through the journey one day at a time. This is the heart of nutrient one.

When leaders forgo their own journeys, they inevitably misread and misappropriate the larger journey of ministry or business. Mark this: Misreading always leads to misleading. How do you learn to read and lead the journey of your team? Learn to read and lead your own journey first. Of course there's more to it than that, but nothing's more fundamental. Journey-less leaders are unable to sense the nuances of the team trek and the messages inside those nuances. When this is the case, the journey-less leader reduces team adventure to task completion. Let's call it tasking. Mark it again: Tasking is the result of leadership minus journey.

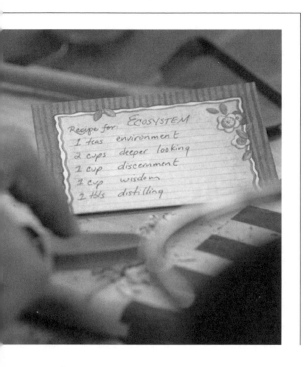

Recipe for: ECOSYSTEM
1 teas   environment
2 cups   deeper looking
1 cup   discernment
1 cup   wisdom
2 tbls   distilling

The first disposition of a leader who journeys is still vision. Vision has taken a beating in the last few years, primarily due to over- and misuse. Leaders of the future will therefore morph it back to its original meaning—the ability to see beneath and perceive what's emerging. For this reason, vision, in the next decade, must move away from vision as a statement on the wall to vision as a wholistic sense, cultivated by both leader and team. Simply, we've got to become seers. The Moses paradigm is dead—it takes the entire team to make the journey of vision.

NUTRIENT TWO: ECOSYSTEM

The best place to discover the reality of nutrient two is at your local pond. This watery wetland is comprised of bacteria, plants, animals, fish, and other surprises. But what makes the pond an ecosystem is more than the fact that all the elements in the pond exist together—they're all interrelated and interdependent. Remove too many elements from the ecosystem, and the life of the entire system is in danger. When thinking about your team and all of its situational layers and loops, it's best to think of it as its own little ecosystem.

We saw in nutrient one just how important the journey is to the effectiveness of a leader. The second leader nutrient localizes the first. Every journey must occur within the confines of a specific time and space. In other words, an adventure needs a place to emerge. The ecosystem of the team is that place. Though you share some similarities with other ecosystems, yours is also distinctive. Your circumstances, situations, and relationships are unique because of how they weave together in everyday occurrences. Understanding leadership theory and practice "in general" isn't enough. You must know how to apply it to your specific context. That means you must first know your environment, and then allow it to thrive rather than control it.

Understanding the interrelationship and interdependency of the team allows a leader to focus his or her vision and energy on the right dynamics. Staff conflict is often the result of something larger than the two people involved in the argument. There are all kinds of other influences at work. Do you know how to read those influences and assist your team to do the same? Learning to read and lead the entire ecosystem of your team is critical to its emerging vision.

NUTRIENT THREE: FREEDOM

Joseph was sold into slavery because of a dream. Joan of Arc was imprisoned for her integrity. Neo was trapped in the matrix. If there's one universal theme in all stories, it's that the character faces a burden, prison, or resistance of some sort. Can you think of a good story where this isn't the case? Yet the reality of burdens and bondages isn't reserved for stories. It can also be found in the stories of the people whom you lead and in your own life. Each person has a prison or a burden from which he or she is seeking release.

The paradox of snares is that at one moment they thwart our journey, our becoming, while in the next, as we learn to press through them, they enable us to reach a greater sense of freedom and growth. Think about it; without snares there'd be no freedom to find.

I'm convinced that the difference between a snare that remains a trap and one that leads to freedom is relationship. In every good story, the trapped character always needs the help of others to find freedom. Jean Vanier, close friend of Henri Nouwen, once wrote in *Becoming Human*, "Belonging is important for our growth to independence; even further, it is important for our growth to inner freedom and maturity. It is only through belonging that we can break out of the shell of individualism and self-centeredness that both protects and isolates."

Nutrient one reminds us that life's a journey. This means that each person in your ecosystem (nutrient two) is on a journey. Now I'm suggesting that each person's journey includes prisons, burdens, and traps. Leaders are in a unique position to help others find freedom through the power of relationship. Work, including work in the church, has for too long centered on a utilitarian approach to relationship. Relationships are developed because in doing so, work can be accomplished more effectively. In other words, the relationships are only as pertinent as the bottom line—whatever the bottom line happens to be. It may sound like semantics or pie-in-the-sky theory, but here's the truth: Relationships precede work and ministry. Genuine belonging precedes consistent and potent communal expression. In other words, the real power of a team enlarges as their relationships deepen.

All of this could sound as though I'm suggesting that leaders are to be a cross between Peter Drucker and Mother Teresa— solving every organizational problem and healing every personal wound. Not even close. Remember in nutrient one we discovered that the vision of the team is probably in the team, more than in the leader. Well, it's true in nutrient three as well. The healing and freedom people need doesn't have to come only from the leader. In fact, great leaders look to engage the team in helping each other to freedom. Remember the healing and team effectiveness you are seeking will flow out of relationship and friendship. Nutrient three doesn't remove the need for healthy boundaries at work, but rather taps the power of the team to bring freedom to the individual. In the long run, a healthier individual means a healthier team.

NUTRIENT FOUR: STEWARDSHIP

I've always been fascinated by quilts. Of particular interest to me is the communal quilt. Communal quilts require each quilter to bring his or her square to the group, and then together the squares become a larger work of art. Yet the true artistry occurs when they're "drawn together." The process of sewing the quilt squares together is a great picture of nutrient four: stewardship.

Leaders are stewards. They're responsible for drawing the team together in order to unleash its artistry. Using the word "stewardship," however, requires some further explanation. One thing's for sure, we've got to get an older version of stewardship out of our minds—fast! In his book, *The Circle of Innovation* (Random House), Tom Peters writes these radical words (when aren't Peters' words radical?):

"The leader of anything has traditionally been thought of as a steward. That's a superb and moral idea. It's also a conservative notion. Or at least that's the way it has traditionally been translated. Conventional wisdom: Steward = Conservator. I still buy the idea of stewardship. In fact, I think it's more important than ever. But…I don't think steward-as-conservator works anymore. She or he is now responsible for living a new message…IF IT AIN'T BROKE, BREAK IT (OR SOMEBODY ELSE WILL BREAK IT FOR YOU!)"

Suffice to say, when I use the word "stewardship" throughout this nutrient, I'm not referring to a milquetoast approach to leadership. Stewards have to learn that drawing people together is a more ambiguous, chaotic (in the good sense), and unpredictable process than the conventional ideas of steward afford.

DREAMING REALITY: THE OVER-THE-RAINBOW LEADER

Over-the-rainbow leader—now that's a good description of a leader-steward. Let me explain. The leader of today and tomorrow must be a steward of the emerging organizational or communal dream and purpose. This means they're cultivating the ability to see and perceive the vision (nutrient one) of the ecosystem (nutrient two). They're able to perceive what hasn't yet emerged and pull people together in order to accomplish that unseen dream. The O.T.R.L. makes over-the-rainbow dreams here and now realities. But they don't do it by themselves. In fact, they know just how important everyone else is to the dream—and the reality. But it takes more than forecasting to bring about this dream; it takes stewardship.

To steward a 21st-century church or organization requires the leader to embrace a systems approach to leadership. This takes us back to the ecosystem. Peter Senge, organizational learning guru, helped us see the value of systems thinking and practice in his landmark book, *The Fifth Discipline* (Doubleday). The question now becomes how to create and unleash—good stewarding words—an ecosystem that's aware of its power to learn, innovate, and collaborate. To wit, I'd suggest three roles for the 21st-century leader-steward.

Transmitter of Wisdom: Unleashing the system through wisdom transmission.

Instigator of Curiosity: Unlearning the system so it's open to new ideas born out of curiosity.

Instigator of Process: Uncovering the system's rigid routines and encouraging new processes.

NUTRIENT FIVE: CHAOS AND CREATIVITY

"Oh, man, have I been there"—situation one: Imagine one of the members of your team comes to you with both a difficult situation and a bad attitude. The person, demanding and frustrated, begins to share his or her woes. As you listen you realize the person has a legitimate point. The problem is, you don't have a clue how to fix the problem—and frankly, the person is starting to get on your nerves. Now you're starting to get angry.

"Oh man, have I been there"—situation two: You're in a meeting where your authority as a leader is being challenged. The challenge is growing more intense as you try to make your case. The others in the meeting notice the tension mounting, and the room grows awkward. You have the authority to simply silence the person or overpower the dissenter by position or knowledge. Should you?

As a leader, the scenarios above are not fictitious in nature. They're everyday realities. What's a leader to do when everything within and without seems to block advancement? Why are more situations failing to yield to my control as a leader? These are the kinds of questions we face in the final nutrient. These are the questions of chaos and creativity.

Chaos—the word conjures up negative images of reckless confusion. Listen to the way we use the word: "It was total chaos." "I can't take this chaotic relationship." This is an unfortunate, but rather embedded definition of chaos. *Chaos* has become a negative word synonymous with things like confusion and disaster. Yet chaos and confusion are worlds apart. When we equate chaos with confusion, it leads to a natural conclusion: Chaos is something to be avoided. This conclusion leads to all kinds of problems, not to mention the most basic problem, which is that we foster an unwillingness to embrace the very things that bring creative energy to the surface. As individuals and leaders, it's time to reinvent this word and renew our commitment to a relationship with chaos. Oh yes,

I'm serious—embrace it like a friend. If you do, it will introduce you to other friends such as ambiguity, paradox, mystery, and surrender—all of whom you need to know if you want to be an innovative leader in the decades ahead.

The universe, Genesis tells us, was created out of chaos. "The Spirit hovered over the formless void," (the chaos). Out of this chaos, God spoke things into existence. I like to imagine this as energy and matter emerging out of the swirling chaos, and forming itself into the spoken command of God. Each vibration of God's Word manifested a newly created thing: light, darkness, plants, trees, water, fish, people, and a host of other created beings. It's interesting to consider that God chose to use chaos when creating the world. Obviously we don't have the details of how this took place, but one thing is clear: chaos was part of the design.

Formless and void—does that describe your life, or at least parts of it? How, our response—as leaders—to it is. When chaos arises on my team, if I panic (seeing it as an enemy), it will shut down the creative process. In times of uncertainty, leaders often trade in creative chaos for a false stability. Stability never comes from removing chaos. Rather it comes from the creative structures that emerge out of the chaos. Often, when we look back at chaotic times, we see that creativity and meaning came as a result of that season.

Leaders tend to hurry to order and structure. "I will feel better and the team will produce more if control is exerted"—wrong. No, this is more than wrong, it's the enemy of true creativity. And if you think I'm kidding, just start micromanaging more of your team and see what you get. Controlling things and people is the primary mistake we make when chaos comes knocking. We try to manipulate people and situations in order to ease the feelings that accompany the chaos. We rush toward the wrong things. Remember what the Spirit did at creation. The Spirit hovered. The word *hover* doesn't suggest a resolution for resolution's sake. But rather it suggests a relaxed, but intentional participation with the chaos.

Twenty-first century leaders will understand the power of finding the pattern of creativity hidden in the chaos and amplifying that pattern as it emerges. You don't control chaos; you co-create out of it with God. Think of an area of chaos currently at work on your team. Has your control of the situation brought about what you desire? Rather than eliminating chaos, try to find a creative possibility that's hidden in it. Now all the nutrients come together to help you discover the next part of the vision swirling in the chaos. Is this cool or what? What a great adventure God has placed before us!

LOW-FAT, HIGH NUTRIENT

It won't be long. After you put this article down, you'll be faced with a leadership moment. The question is, do you have the vitality to meet the challenge? Part of what creates that vitality is your leadership diet. Keep it low in fat and high in the five nutrients. When you come across good leadership information, ask yourself which of the five nutrients you can store it in for later retrieval. Soon, you'll find you have more resilience, endurance, and flexibility as a leader. Just what the leader ordered!

NEVER STOP LEARNING

by PAUL ALLEN | *(September/October 2002)*

Not too long ago, I had the opportunity to participate in a small class titled "The Church and The Postmodern Culture." In all honesty, I wasn't expecting anything out of the ordinary, especially considering the amount of available conferences, books, and other resources regarding the same topic. However, I was pleasantly surprised and encouraged by the class instructor.

Our instructor, Richard Cox, is an author, psychologist, physician, theologian, former school president, charter member of the American Association of Pastoral Counselors, and an ordained minister. Add to that an accomplished musician and artist, and you have a postmodern renaissance man. And although all of that is worthy of note, the thing that impressed me the most is his ability to investigate and question current and popular

thought as well as identify his need to change—and doing so at 74 years of age.

Wow, I thought I was pretty flexible and a lifelong learner. What I discovered was there are things—practices and methods—that I still hold on to pretty strongly, defying anyone to question them or suggest something else.

Then I had an opportunity to attend a speedway on a trip to Michigan. The owner of the racetrack was in his late 70s, and in my conversation with one of the drivers I learned that he, too, was constantly looking at ways to improve his facilities and make his customers more welcome. On a side note, it was interesting to see him meeting and greeting people as they arrived and departed, noting his infectious charm that affected many of the 4,000-plus attendees.

A few weeks later, I was admiring the paintings of an artist at a community art show. Later as I looked at her Web site, I read that the artist—again in her 70s—has continued to let her style evolve to reflect her lifestyle and the culture in which she lives.

My point? I know I'm being challenged by these intersections in life to be more of a life-long learner and to never think I'm too old to learn something new. Regarding the deeper ramifications, I'm still pondering it myself. Shouldn't we as pastors and leaders be on a continual journey of learning? Shouldn't we be appalled with the status quo? Shouldn't our ministry look different today than it did a few years ago? Shouldn't we be the influencers of change—positive change in our world—instead of letting the world influence us?

The obvious application is there: As life-long learners, our love for Christ should increase and we should strive to be people of the Word. But what about the not so obvious—being willing to change our methods and practices—not our message and foundation? Perhaps we might start looking at the church, the world, and our influence in a whole new light with unique opportunities to share the good news.

Let's take the lead from these vibrant seniors and live life with passion, observe the culture, and change when necessary, that our world may experience the love of God.

KALEIDOSCOPIC LEADERSHIP

by RON MARTOIA | *(March/April 2001)*

ka•lei•do•scope: Gr. kalos, beautiful + eidos, form—anything that constantly changes as in color and pattern.

Are you constantly creating a place of discovery and belonging?

Several years ago I remember reading for the first time what's now a well-known definition of *leadership* by Max DePree, "The first responsibility of a leader is to define reality." I was soon asking myself what proved to be painfully hard questions: "As a leader, what kind of reality do I help define? What about for our lead team? our board? our core of unpaid servants?" These were painful questions because the discovery didn't provoke much celebration, and they're hard questions because defining, creating, and architecting reality is no easy task.

Initially I had a soaring confidence about this issue. My '90s "conference junkie" mindset convinced me there must be some program, clergy update tape club, or defining moment I needed to have to get this figured out. Over time, however, I concluded I had no idea how to do this or what my desired outcome would be.

In the ensuing years, I've come to a major ah-ha. While the point leader is usually the primary creative communicator, the team catalyst, and even possibly the chief brain-juice hydrant, we must be much, much more. We must be ambience architects, sculptors of organizational culture, gardeners of organic life.

As leaders we must germinate and catalyze the dance of colorful pieces in the kaleidoscope we call church ethos. Ethos is the tangible yet invisible "space-feel" that you immediately experience every time you walk into a church. Ethos is what's found to be compelling and inviting or cool and repelling to those who walk through the doorway. What space-feel are we designing? What kind of environment are we creating where the dance of others' gifts, God's Spirit, the mess of new birth, and the depth of encountering God can all come together in a kaleidoscope of color?

Our postmodern world is screaming for a real-life experience of transformation, an encounter with the divine, and something to satiate its ferocious appetite for community. We live in a new day. We all sense it. We read about it and we even conference on it. But the question remains: Will we as church leaders spawn life within the organismic ethos of church—life so compelling that people simply can't stay away?

To use Eugene Peterson's translation from *The Message*, will we present to the lost among us a "more and better life than they ever dreamed of" (John 10:10)?

As I began wrestling with these issues, I realized I was ill-prepared and untrained to ride this transitional cusp of history. There were certain dispositions, certain mirrors in my personal kaleidoscope that needed to be present and rightly placed if I was going to lead our teams into a healthy ethos. Being a bit slow on the uptake at times, this stands as one of the most critical insights for me about leadership and its connection to ethos. The condition, vitality, health, and movement in a local church can't be understood apart from the condition, vitality, health, and movement of its leaders. Are there exceptions? Sure. But this fundamental and profound truth still remains. In my life and in the life of all leaders, their spiritual dynamic, clarity of vision, and level of expectancy usually play out in a near one-to-one correspondence in the teams we serve and then into the larger group of the church as a whole. Interestingly, over the last six to eight years this insight has risen to the forefront of secular literature on leadership.

In a traditional kaleidoscope, three small mirrors provide the surface where small pieces of different colored glass or plastic dance. Three mirrors also need to be present in our leadership life if we hope to provide an ethos where the compelling dance of color can occur.

MIRROR #1: INTERIOR SPACE LEADERSHIP

The exterior space around us is directly contoured and shaped by the condition of our interior space. When we think of leading, rarely does personal self-leadership come flooding into our minds. We almost always think about leading people who we consider subordinates or followers. Dee Hock, founder of Visa International, stated in "The Art of Chaordic Leadership" (*Leader to Leader*) that as key leaders we should be spending no less than 50 percent of our time on personal self-leadership issues.

I don't need to look very far in my history to note that when my local church—Westwinds—struggled, it was often because I was struggling. When I was going through some growing up on the inside, Westwinds was directly affected. When I experienced a quantum surge and God grew me, most often our teams as a whole felt it. This simple truth rocked my world: What happens in us as leaders will eventually contour and animate what happens around us. What's going on inside us will ultimately leak out to those around us. This is why you and I can't be shy about focusing on the interior space mirror.

What kind of things are interior space leadership issues? In an article that was the most requested Harvard Business Review article in 1999, Daniel Goleman says that as important as technical job know-how and IQ are in a leader's performance, what he calls emotional intelligence is more than two times more important in leaders at all levels of an organization. He says its importance increases as a leader's responsibilities rise. Emotional intelligence is interior space leadership stuff.

Self-awareness, self-regulation, motivation, empathy, social skill—this is the stuff of deep maturity and character development. How much have you wrestled with these issues in your own personal leadership development? How much time have you spent exploring, developing, and honing these kinds of emotional intelligence skills?

And this is just the beginning. What about learning to build on islands of health and strength—a rather counterintuitive approach, but one that all great leaders are aware of? What about really being mentored in terms of gift development—and what that means to your internal self-perceptions about how God's made you and who he wants you to become?

This personal mirror will help shape a church ethos of life development and health hunger. Few things are more compelling than watching authentic growth and maturity evolve in others. Every time I see someone go deeper, deal with some emotional growing up, or take a character issue to the next level, I get inspired. When a group of leaders get the mirror of interior space leadership in place, powerful stuff slowly leaks into the ethos of the church. People will observe imperfect but growing leaders and will long for the same in their lives. The interior space leadership mirror animates a life development and health hunger ethos in the church.

MIRROR #2: RELENTLESS CURIOSITY

Every great leader I've observed or read about has an unyielding curiosity. I'm personally convinced this has to fuel lifelong learning. Those '90s conferences we attended did tell us we needed to be lifelong learners, that leaders are learners, that leaders are readers. No doubt true! But what fuels lifelong learning?

Without curiosity informing our questions, piquing our interest, or pondering the "what-ifs," lifelong learning may be nothing but an excuse for evidence gathering to justify and calcify the status quo. Information influx isn't a transformation experience.

Several areas of curiosity should be the constant companions of leaders.

1. CURIOSITY ABOUT SPIRITUAL FORMATION

- *What's God doing in my spirit and what's he going to do next?*
- *How's God going to keep soul-silt to a minimum in my spirit, and what's my role?*
- *How's freshness going to stay continual in my spiritual life, and how do I also facilitate that in the lives of my teammates?*

2. CURIOSITY ABOUT AREAS OUTSIDE OUR FRAME OF KNOWLEDGE

- *Extraordinary leaders almost universally read, inquire, take classes, and learn from people who are doing things in arenas totally outside their realm of expertise or interest.*
- *Have you ever thought about reading a book on Leonardo daVinci? He's considered the greatest genius to date. How about Picasso, Gandhi, or Churchill?*
- *When was the last time you thought about picking up a piece on bio-technology or the mapping of the genome project and probing what's going on in the area of cloning and genetic engineering? These topics will have significant implications for cultural penetration and how the gospel may impact decision making.*
- *Have you ever thought about how colors impact people's life and environment? What about smells?*

A relentless curiosity about random areas outside our frame

is one of the things that allow great leaders to make creative connections among things that previously might not have been connected. A mentor challenged this in my life several years ago, and now it's a benchmark of my life.

3. CURIOSITY ABOUT OUR CULTURE

- *How does postmodern culture impact our ministry paradigms and assumptions right now?*
- *How are we going to understand and engage the arena of ideas in such a way that we have hearing as a Christian church?*

When this second mirror of relentless curiosity takes its place in the life of leaders, a couple of things slowly leak into the ethos of the church. People come to expect that new, creative, and fresh ways of doing things will be sought and expected. The ethos of the church becomes one of permission-giving innovation. Ideas from the margins are seen as not only acceptable but greatly desired and appreciated. Curiosity yielding lifelong learning in leaders essentially creates an innovative ethos, a culture where "the new thing" (Isaiah 43:19) God may want to do is explored and celebrated. Not only do the kaleidoscopic pieces dance with innovation, but resilience and "risk readiness" also join the dance. In my context, this is an incredible blessing. From our highly unusual and artistic facility to the off-the-wall ideas we try in our Encounter and Fusion weekend services, our ethos is that of adaptability and excitement over the new. As the spiritual and cultural tectonic plates continue to shift under our feet, risk, resilience, and innovation become increasingly important. The Apostle Paul is the quintessential pragmatist and innovator when he essentially said: "I will constantly morph maverick methods if that is what it takes to win a few" (1 Corinthians 9:19-23).

We're absolutely convinced that the best ways of reaching the lost, growing deep teenagers, assisting the broken to reach wholeness, and connecting our community to a relationship with Jesus they simply can't live without, have yet to be designed, sketched, and sculpted. Those only represent a few nuggets of rationale for ambience architects who create cultures of wild permission-giving and risky what-if dream sessions. We need to sculpt space where the most direct route between two points is a spiral because the outcome we're seeking isn't determined by the speed of travel.

MIRROR #3: EXPECTATION FOR THE OUTRAGEOUS

Jesus did little in Scripture that was pedestrian or mundane. That isn't to say that most of what he did was sensational. However, Jesus was full of the unexpected, the arresting, the unanticipated. This is the third mirror of kaleidoscopic leadership. Do we really subscribe to an Ephesians 3:20 expectation, "…who is able to do immeasurably more than all we can ask or imagine"? Do we as leaders genuinely go around with full expectation that the unexpected may break in?

My first sense that this mirror was absent from my kaleidoscopic repertoire was when, in the space of two weeks, God answered with clarity and tremendous power a number of huge requests. I was dumbfounded and totally shocked. I'm ashamed to say the profound lesson to emerge was that my expectation level with God's activity was near the zero mark. His consistent, unexpected, and outrageous breaking into my life in that two-week period was an essential indictment of my faith level. An obvious question ensues. If my level of expectation was so low, was it any wonder our teams in our church ethos-at-large would also have a low expectation level?

Our pre-Christian culture is full of people disillusioned with self-designed deities. They're tired of the manageable manipulability of gods of their making. Many of them are ready for a God-sized God. The question we must ask is, is that the kind of God we're introducing them to—a God of biblical proportion?

Kaleidoscopic leadership requires the personal mirrors of interior space leadership, relentless curiosity, and an expectation for the outrageous. When these personal mirrors are in place, they slowly yield a church ethos of life development, innovation and risk-taking, and an

KALEIDOSCOPIC QUESTIONS

1. When was the last time you reflected on your expectation level? How would you rate it?

2. When was the last time the church got extravagant with its trust and saw God really do something beyond human ability?

3. What can you do to breed an ethos of outrageous expectation?

outrageous expectation that God can and will do anything. If Max DuPree is right—that the first responsibility of a leader is to define reality—I can think of few realities we'd rather see dance in the kaleidoscope.

SOAK UP SPIRITUAL DIRECTION

"God's heart is the most sensitive and tender of all. No act goes unnoticed, no matter how insignificant or small."

—RICHARD J. FOSTER

SERVANT LEADERS

by ALAN NELSON | *(May/June 2000)*

In his book *Servant Leadership*, Robert Greenleaf said, "To become a servant leader, you must first become a servant." The idea is one of self-image—how we see ourselves.

The servant is a person whose job is to serve others. Naturally, you can serve others without the attitude of a servant, which is servility. Servant-like behavior without a servant-like attitude is little more than parroting submissive behavior. A person who sees herself as a leader who serves others isn't nearly as dynamic as a person who sees herself as a servant who leads as a tool to serve. A servant's ambition is to help other people. Jesus used his powers to heal, his teaching gifts to instruct, and a towel and basin to wash feet. A servant will use whatever gifts are at her disposal to serve others.

When a servant recognizes the gift of leading as an available tool, she'll in turn use leading to serve others. When not leading, the servant leader's self-image doesn't change, because leading is just a tool, not an identity.

Servant leaders must realize that their primary tool for service is leading. Moses had a servant's heart, but he was serving poorly in Exodus 18 because he was trying to counsel everyone instead of developing an organization to serve the masses. He'd neglected his most potent tool for service—leading. The world's in great need of people who are true servants, men and women who use the tool of leading to serve organizations, ministries, and community groups.

If one person above, below, and at your level would rate you in these three areas, how would you fare? Try this evaluation.

On a scale of 1 to 5, with five being the highest, rate yourself as a:

_____ servant

_____ leader

_____ servant leader

HOW'S YOUR VISION?
Improving Your Leadership From Conception to Implementation

by DARREN WALTER | *(March/April 2003)*

Several months ago, I came to the conclusion—with the encouragement of my wife—that it was time for some new glasses. Odds were pretty good that my prescription lenses were as out of date as my frames were. So the next Saturday we went to the optometrist together. My exam began with the usual preliminaries, an eye measurement here, a glaucoma test there, and the ever-popular eye chart exam.

"Okay, Darren," the lady in the white lab coat announced. "Let's see how well you do reading these letters without your glasses."

Without my specs, this was destined to be an embarrassing situation. I took one squinty look at the chart and immediately asked for the English version.

"Just do your best," she encouraged, as my wife giggled in the background.

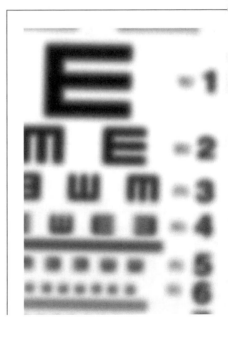

"E!" I exclaimed proudly. They can't trick me. I can pick out a three-foot tall letter E anywhere. Now the rest of the letters were going to be a bit more challenging. Contorting my face into a thousand different shapes, I squinted and strained my way through the next line or two. Occasionally my wife, Amanda, could be heard in the background trying to muffle her laughter mixed with pity.

"You really are blind, aren't you?" Amanda whispered.

And then, with a twinge of competition in her voice, the lady in the white lab coat asked, "How's your vision, Amanda?"

You don't know what you're getting into, I thought to myself. *Amanda has 20/20 vision. She'll smoke this wimpy eye chart in a second!* Knowing that the attention was off my eyesight and the possibility of having my driver's license revoked, I relaxed and watched Amanda read the same chart from four feet behind me.

Like reading the ingredients off the back of a can of alphabet soup, Amanda fired off a rapid stream of letters. After she finished reading the bottom paragraph of fine print, including the copyright disclaimer, date issued, and the U.S. patent number, a deafening silence fell over the exam lobby. The white lab coat lady knew she'd been beaten. She smiled at Amanda and reluctantly bestowed on her the nickname *Show-Off.* Amanda smiled back and wore the title like a badge of honor. Glancing my way, the nice lady picked up my chart, turned toward the hallway and said, "Follow me, Squinty."

So there we were…Squinty and Show-Off. As similar as my wife and I are in many ways, we didn't see eye-to-eye when it came to eyesight. This side of heaven, I probably won't have 20/20 vision like Amanda. Lucky for me, I was in the right place. I was at the optometrist's office. My far-less-than-perfect vision can be enhanced. Some people would leave the doctor's office that day with contacts, some having received a special treatment, some scheduled for corrective surgery, and some with glasses like myself. Hopefully, everyone would leave with improved vision.

Often I spend time admiring people with great vision. However, I'm not talking about the 20/20s of the optometry hall of fame. I'm talking about the visionaries of this world—those who see what no one else sees or has the courage to admit they see it: the Wright Brothers, the Walt Disneys, the Bill Gateses of this world. I think of the missionaries and church planters that have stepped out in faith and vision. Where would we be today without people of vision? Where would the church be today without visionaries?

Just as my experience in the exam area of the optometrist's illustrated, not everyone has the same quality of vision. The same is clearly true of vision in the spiritual sense. Some people have 20/20 vision. These visionaries look at a piece of property and see a state-of-the-art church facility by a future bustling freeway. They glance at an abandoned warehouse in the most dangerous part of the city and see a thriving outreach center. They meet a backward

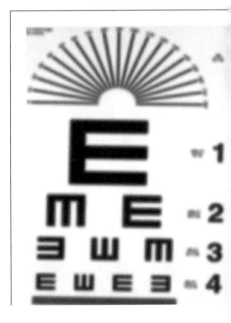

teenager with Coke-bottle glasses and see the heart of the next Billy Graham. For the rest of us who lack that sharp and polished ability to envision what could be, there's hope. There are steps we can take to improve our vision.

PRAYER AND PRESENTATION

Prayer isn't the obligatory first step in any spiritual list, nor is it the magic piece of the puzzle we must include if we want God to nod his head in approval. Prayer is our singular means of communication with the Vision-Giver. It's our chance to present our deepest desires and requests to God. As Philippians 4:6 reminds us, "Do not be anxious about anything [vision included], but in everything, by prayer and petition, with thanksgiving, present your requests to God." Prayer is also a great place to hear a presentation or two from God himself.

Where does your vision originate? Did your Maker plant your vision deep inside you? Is God softly whispering a vision in your ear, or are you shouting your own plan to drown out his voice? These questions must be answered before your vision can be a reality. If your vision has originated with God as its source, if God planted a vision deep within you, if he's whispering his vision for your life and your soul resonates with the sound of his voice, then you must talk with the God of vision. Prayer is our link with the mastermind of the universe. Through prayer we align our plans, feelings, and desires with our Father. Prayer is our opportunity to consult with the most visionary being in existence.

The One who envisioned endless galaxies, deep oceans, and microscopic cells wants to share with you the many visions he has for your life, from the tiny to the eternal. The One who had a vision for the human heart and a vision for how to redeem it is anxious to develop heart-to-heart communication with you. The One whose visions created a world of realities as profound as its mysteries is willing to share the secrets of vision with you.

Prayer is the perfect context to present your ideas and visions to God. In prayer, measure your plans against his will. Present your vision before him, and then give him free reign to change it, enhance it, obliterate it, or smile upon it.

If you skip prayer and presentation to God and can complete your vision on your own, the vision isn't worth the investment. Calling on God and quietly listening to his voice in prayer and presentation is where vision begins, struggles, and eventually grows to completion.

FLEXIBILITY AND FAITHFULNESS

If we're not careful, our vision can become tunnel vision. It's easy for pride of ownership to creep into our plans. We can become so invested and focused on a particular dream or vision that we begin to see no other possibility, no other way. The genesis of a vision isn't the time to put on blinders. Even after our vision takes shape and becomes a reality, there still must be room for change and modification.

How often do we look like narrow-minded children to God? We're often like a child who sees only one use for his toy. *This toy car was meant to be pounded on*, the child's developing mind reasons. All the while, the child's unaware that the toy car will putt all around the room, make real car noises, and even respond to the child's verbal commands. When we pigeonhole our vision, we're only limiting the greatness of God.

Our flexibility is necessary if we want the vision to not only be accomplished, but to also result in more than we imagined. Flexibility is difficult because it proves we aren't in charge. Flexibility says there may be a better way. It admits there could be more to this than we originally thought. Our willingness to be flexible when it comes to vision is directly tied to whether we see God as our irreplaceable partner or as an aggravating distraction to our plans.

Flexibility is a wonderful byproduct of faith. It illustrates that faith in God will smooth out the vision's rough edges. An attitude of flexibility is evidence that it may take time and must take God to see the plan come to completion. Realistically, all visions don't grow from conception to maturity overnight. Faithfulness will be our greatest asset in the days, months, or years between the vision's beginning and end. We'll often be tempted to let pride push the vision through and insist it's

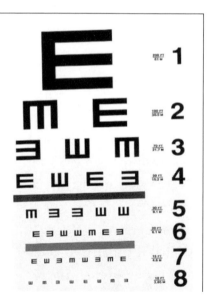

done our way. Don't give in. "The Lord preserves the faithful, but the proud he pays back in full" (Psalm 31:23).

The sailor's faithfulness from wave's crest to crest is what gets him to shore. Serving faithfully, even when it appears the vision is lost at sea, will make all the difference. Our faithfulness in the vision-valleys will make the high peaks that much sweeter. Faithfulness through the journey of vision will please God and deepen our resolve and devotion to him. Faithfully follow him whether the vision is alive, dead, or painfully slipping away. Freely loosen the grip on the vision to allow God the flexibility to enhance and shape the final result. Step by step, from devastation to victory, the right, God-honoring vision will surface.

SIMMERING AND SHARING

How many times have you poured out your heart of vision only to have it stepped on by someone who just didn't get it? I'm much too anxious. The second I think God's given me a vision or idea, I can't wait to share it. I not only want to serve it to everyone, I want to force-feed them my vision. However, I'm learning there's real value in letting your vision simmer for a season.

When we're trying to let our vision simmer, it seems as though the rest of the world's driving full speed ahead and we're left covered in their cloud of dust and exhaust. In the early emotion of vision, it's easy to think everyone else is succeeding while you're left standing. "Be still before the Lord and wait patiently for him; do not fret when men succeed in their ways…" (Psalm 37:7). Don't be discouraged. Allow the dust to settle and the fumes to drift away. Remember, even the best vision at the wrong time will fail. God's timing is always best.

Think of the dramatic difference simmering makes in the life of something as ordinary as soup. When you first toss the ingredients into the pot, the soup is certainly edible but not very desirable. However, after the ingredients simmer together for hours, the finished product's not only edible, but depending on the chef, it could be masterful. Could your vision benefit from simmer time? Allow God to combine the ingredients of your gifts, personality, and experiences to create a vision for your life. He's an excellent chef and loves to toss in the special secret ingredients and spices that will turn your vision into a masterpiece. Allow your journey of vision to deepen your relationship with God. Keep the vision a simmering secret for a while, just between you and the One who knows you best. Don't be too anxious to lift the lid. Be careful not to spoil the moment when God says it's time to unveil what you've been working on together.

Once the master chef says enough simmering has taken place, enjoy sharing the joint creation with a hungry crowd. It may be wise to share the vision with a select, trusted few before serving it to the masses. Anticipation builds in a house where soup is simmering over time. Allow God to create an environment of anticipation, eager for the mouth-watering possibilities of the savory vision.

Thinking back on that visit with my wife to the optometrist, I can't help but appreciate her seeing superiority. It's obvious that she earned the nickname Show-Off as much as I earned the nickname Squinty. When it comes to vision, it's equally as obvious that it comes naturally for some while others have to hone the ability. Compared to God, the ultimate Vision-caster, all of us fall miserably short. Aren't you grateful we have a patient and willing teacher, eager to share with us the wonder and awe of what could be if we only trust him? With a grin God looks at each of us, motions forward into his vast imagination and invites, "Follow me, Squinty."

SENSING GOD'S ABSENCE

by PAUL ALLEN | *(May/June 2005)*

It's interesting to think about the number of times during the week we talk about sensing God's presence, wanting to see the Holy One's work in our midst, asking him to bless our ministries, and sending him multiple other requests.

I've been wondering if sometimes we're so busy planning, programming, and proceeding toward our goals that perhaps we move forward without God being present in the plans, programs, and goals.

I was rereading the story of Mary and Martha in Luke 10:38-42 and noticed something that made me stop. I've read the passage several times, always being drawn to the fact that Martha was angry because she was doing all the work while Mary sat and listened to Jesus. Like Martha, we're so busy doing things we forget the "one thing" that Mary understood—to be in relationship with Jesus.

This time I was struck by something I had never seen before. Martha was busy doing things for Jesus. However, even though he was in the same house, she didn't sense his absence from her list of projects. How odd. Jesus was there in her house and all she can think about is everything that has to be done.

I joke all the time about being a "Martha" instead of a "Mary," but I think for the first time the Holy Spirit really grabbed my attention. How many times have I prayed for God's presence to be in the midst of something I'm doing and in reality he's already there, just not in the way I expected? Perhaps it has nothing to do with doing, saying, or showing. Maybe it's just about being.

Here at Group Publishing we talk a lot about The 1 Thing®—growing in our relationship with Jesus. I'm reminded—again—that my relationship with God is not about God doing things for me and me doing things for God. It's first about just hanging out together, being friends with God.

What does this mean for us as pastors? Glad you asked. If we believe that leadership "leaks," are we leaking anything to our congregation about spending time with God, just being in the presence of our Friend? Or are we leaking that our top priority is to be busy doing things for God? If we read the story of Mary and Martha in context of pastoral ministry, might we wake up one day tired and angry with God because we've been so busy doing things for God that we missed out on The 1 Thing?

I recently heard about a Christian musician who took a few weeks off to determine God's will for her ministry. She prayed, read the Word, and diligently sought God's direction. Toward the end, she let God know her frustration in not sensing God's presence. At that moment she sensed God asking her if it wasn't enough that they just spent time together.

What about you? Is it time for you to consider that perhaps you've been so busy you haven't noticed God's absence in that "stuff"? Let's stop, and take time just to be present with God.

YOUR LEADERSHIP STYLE AND PREACHING

by ROBERT JOHNSON | *(May/June 2005)*

For those who lead in the context of pastoral ministry, preaching is an obviously vital tool for the task of leadership. Or is it so obvious, really?

On the one hand, your preaching reflects your leadership. Manipulative leaders tend to manipulate people in preaching. If you're a controlling leader who attempts to preach in an empowering way, you will only achieve the result of being thought of as a dishonest, controlling leader. If you're a timid, "spineless" leader, your attempt at bold, courageous preaching will probably be interpreted as either passive-aggression or a carefully crafted performance. Although some preachers attempt to do so, preaching cannot "cover up" your leadership approach. However, when there's consistency between your approach to preaching and your leadership style, you increase the level of integrity for your entire life and ministry.

On the other hand, preaching can greatly support your leadership. The preaching moment is always a time to set out the vision of God's will for the congregation. Therefore, in reality, good preaching is always good leading.

Good preaching connects with people. The preacher is in touch with people's hurts, pains, hopes, fears, and aspirations. The good preacher has the ability to connect with people in such a way that they feel that their preacher "lives on their street." Connecting is the first step to good leading.

Good preaching provokes a creative dissatisfaction with current conditions. The preacher is able to accurately, passionately, and incisively describe a present situation that leads people to a place of saying, "something needs to be done about that!"

Good preaching envisions a preferred future. Preachers from the past described heaven as the preferred future. While that's certainly "fair game," good preaching envisions a preferred future that includes a better life for people in the "here and now" and in all the places of their lives where they need real transformation.

Finally, good preaching motivates people to action. Beyond the description of a problem or the vision of a preferred future, good preaching inspires, encourages, and evokes meaningful action. Good preaching is a catalyst for positive change, and gets people motivated to move their feet in that meaningful mission.

REMEMBER YOUR CALLING

by PAUL ALLEN | *(September/October 2005)*

In today's ministry world, we often hear so much about leadership that we forget what we've been called to do—pastor. As pastors, we need to be reminded what Jesus said in John 21:15-19: "Feed my lambs...take care of my sheep...feed my sheep."

Instead of always picking up the latest book on leadership to improve your ministry, why don't you go back and do a word study on what it means to pastor?

Let's take another look at the word *shepherd*.

Find all the verses that mention *shepherd*, print them out, and do a personal evaluation. For example, look at 1 Peter 5:2-3: "Be shepherds of God's flock that is under your care, serving as overseers—not because you must, but because you are willing, as God wants you to be; not greedy for money, but eager to serve; not lording it over those entrusted to you, but being examples to the flock."

Do this with different verses throughout the Scriptures that give us examples of how to pastor. When you combine this with what you've learned from the latest book, conference, or conversation, imagine what new things God might do in your ministry.

Then work through the following questions alone or with your pastor friends:

1. What are shepherds and what are shepherds willing to do for their flock?

2. What does it mean to serve as an overseer? Are you a willing overseer?

3. Are you eager to serve? Or are you "eager for money"? or power? or prestige? or the love of others?

4. Are you an example to the flock? Do people see you as one who "lords" or someone who's an example of Christ?

5. Can you write down examples of where you've lived a life that reflects this Scripture in your own ministry?

Ask God to help you become the type of shepherd described in this passage.

IT'S NOT ABOUT YOU!
A Reminder of God's Purpose for Our Lives

by RICK WARREN | (March/April 2004)

The purpose of your life is far greater than your own personal fulfillment, your peace of mind, or even your happiness. It's far greater than your family, your career, or even your wildest dreams and ambitions. If you want to know why you were placed on this planet, you must begin with God. You were born by his purpose and for his purpose.

The search for the purpose of life has puzzled people for thousands of years. That's because we typically begin at the wrong starting point—ourselves. We ask self-centered questions like: What do I want to be? What should I do with my life? What are my goals, my ambitions, my dreams for my future? But focusing on ourselves will never reveal our life's purpose. The Bible says, "In his hand is the life of every creature and the breath of all mankind" (Job 12:10).

Contrary to what many popular books, movies, and seminars tell you, you won't discover your life's meaning by looking within yourself. You've probably tried that already. You didn't create yourself, so there's no way you can tell yourself what you were created for! If I handed you an invention you had never seen before, you wouldn't know its purpose, and the invention itself wouldn't be able to tell you either. Only the creator or the owner's manual could reveal its purpose.

> *Rev. Thought:* As pastors, it's important for us to remember our purpose as well as be reminded that people in our congregation and community are constantly struggling with finding their purpose in life. An effective guide remembers his or her own struggles.

Bertrand Russell, the famous English atheist, once said, "Unless you assume a God, the question of life's purpose is meaningless." He was correct; if there's no God, then our lives really don't matter. We're just random accidents of nature, and neither our births, our lives, nor our deaths have any meaning or value.

Fortunately, God tells us that we're not accidents and that our lives have significance—because God had his reasons for creating us. The Bible says, "For everything, absolutely everything, above and below, visible and invisible...everything got started in him and finds its purpose in him" (Colossians 1:16, *The Message*).

LET'S START AT THE VERY BEGINNING

I once got lost in the mountains. When I stopped to ask for directions to the campsite, I was told, "You can't get there from here. You must start from the other side of the mountain!"

In the same way, we can't arrive at our life's purpose by starting with a focus on ourselves. We must begin with God, our Creator. We exist only because God wills that we exist. We were made by God and for God—and until we understand that, life will never make sense. It's only in God that we discover our origin, our identity, our meaning, our purpose, our significance, and our destiny. Every other path leads to a dead end.

Many people try to use God for their own self-actualization, but that's a reversal of nature and is doomed to failure. We were made for God, not vice versa, and life is about letting God use us for his purposes, not us using him for our purposes. The Bible says, "Obsession with self in these matters is a dead end; attention to God leads us out into the open, into a spacious, free life" (Romans 8:6, *The Message*).

I've read many books that suggest ways to discover the purpose of my life. All of them could be classified as self-help books because they approach the subject from a self-centered viewpoint. Self-help books, even Christian ones, usually offer the same predictable steps to finding your life's purpose: Consider your dreams. Clarify your values. Set some goals. Figure out what you're good at. Aim high. Go for it! Be disciplined. Believe you can achieve your goals. Involve others. Never give up.

Of course, these recommendations often lead to great success. You can usually succeed in reaching a goal if you put your

> *Rev. Thought:* If you need to, read the last few paragraphs again. Don't get caught in the trap of your sermons sounding like self-help seminars. Make sure you're challenging people to allow God to make a difference in their lives—growing in their relationship with Christ and joining him on their spiritual journey.

mind to it. But being successful and fulfilling your life's purpose are not at all the same issue! You could reach all your personal goals, becoming a raving success by the world's standard, and still miss the purposes for which God created you. You need more than self-help advice. The Bible says, "Self-help is no help at all. Self-sacrifice is the way, my way, to finding yourself, your true self" (Matthew 16:25, *The Message*).

How, then, do you discover the purpose you were created for? You have only two options. Your first option is speculation. This is what most people choose. They conjecture, they guess, they theorize. When people say, "I've always thought life is…" they mean, "This is the best guess I can come up with."

THE MEANING OF LIFE

For thousands of years, brilliant philosophers have discussed and speculated about the meaning of life. Philosophy is an important subject and has its uses, but when it comes to determining the purpose of life, even the wisest philosophers are just guessing.

Hugh Moorhead, a philosophy professor at Northeastern Illinois University, once wrote to 250 of the best-known philosophers, scientists, writers, and intellectuals in the world, asking them, "What is the meaning of life?" He then published their responses in a book. Some offered their best guesses, some admitted that they just made up a purpose for life, and others were honest enough to say they were clueless. In fact, a number of famous intellectuals asked Moorhead to write back and tell them if he discovered the purpose of life!

Fortunately, there's an alternative to speculation about the meaning and purpose of life. It's revelation. We can turn to what God has revealed about life in his Word. The easiest way to discover the purpose of an invention is to ask its creator. The same is true for discovering your life's purpose—ask God.

God hasn't left us in the dark to wonder and guess. He's clearly revealed his five purposes for our lives through the Bible (to worship, to fellowship, to grow in Christ, to serve others, and to share Christ with others).

The Bible is our owner's manual, explaining why we're alive, how life works, what to avoid, and what to expect in the future. It explains what no self-help or philosophy book could know. The Bible says, "God's wisdom...goes deep into the interior of his purposes...It's not the latest message, but more like the oldest—what God determined as the way to bring out his best in us" (1 Corinthians 2:7, *The Message*).

God isn't just the starting point of your life; he's the source of it. To discover your purpose in life you must turn to God's Word, not the world's wisdom. You must build your life on eternal truths, not pop psychology, success-motivation, or inspirational stories. The Bible

Rev. Thought: It's safe for us to realize that no matter how we say it, these five purposes are clearly pointed out in Scripture. Are you using them as a grid for your ministry? Are you making sure that people clearly understand the five purposes—equipping them through whatever means to experience God's best for their lives?

says, "It's in Christ that we find out who we are and what we are living for. Long before we first heard of Christ and got our hopes up, he had his eye on us, had designs on us for glorious living, part of the overall purpose he is working out in everything and everyone" (Ephesians 1:11, *The Message*).

This verse gives us three insights into our purpose:

You discover your identity and purpose through a relationship with Jesus Christ.

God was thinking of you long before you ever thought about him. His purpose for your life predates your conception. He planned it before you existed, without your input! You may choose your career, your spouse, your hobbies, and many other parts of your life, but you don't get to choose your purpose.

The purpose of your life fits into a much larger, cosmic purpose that God has designed for eternity.

Andrei Bitov, a Russian novelist, grew up under an atheistic Communist regime. But God got his attention one dreary day. He recalls, "In my 27th year, while riding the metro in Leningrad (now St. Petersburg) I was overcome with a despair so great that life seemed to stop at once, pre-empting the future entirely, let alone

> *Rev. Thought:* What a great passage for us as pastors. If we understand that our relationship with Jesus began long before we knew him, then we can express through our sermons and lifestyles the reality of God's awesome love and purpose for our lives and the lives of the people we touch.

any meaning. Suddenly, all by itself, a phrase appeared: 'Without God life makes no sense.' Repeating it in astonishment, I rode the phrase up like a moving staircase, got out of the metro, and walked into God's light."

You may have felt as if you're in the dark about your purpose in life. Stop looking within or without, and start looking up—to Jesus Christ and his Word. It's only in Christ that we discover God's five purposes for our lives.

LEADERSHIP IS INFLUENCE

by ROBERT JOHNSON | *(May/June 2004)*

I once heard a pastor tell the story of attending an inner-city event that was an assembly of urban pastors and urban hip-hop music artists. The pastors had planned and organized the conference as an attempt to connect with the hip-hop entertainers who are so influential in creating and shaping the cultures of inner-city lifestyles. During the conference, the pastors criticized the entertainers for their use of vulgar language, their emphasis on sexual promiscuity, and their seemingly constant, verbal denigration of women.

The pastors reminded those entertainers of the fact that many of them had grown up with some kind of connection with the black church, even if only through the prayers of a devoted mother. "Be influenced by your church heritage," the pastors said to the entertainers. Near the end of the event, the pastors, thinking that they'd clearly and decisively made their point, gave opportunity for the entertainers to respond. They were all caught off guard when one of the most well-known among the entertainers stepped to the mic and made one statement: "If you want me to be influenced by you, influence me!"

The entertainer's statement remains with me. If we have no influence with others, that's our burden, not theirs. Of course, I expect the people in the church where I serve to be vulnerable to my influence, at least to some degree. But if I want to influence people in the world, in my community, at the fitness club, then I must bear the burden of my desire to influence.

The church, in general, often seems to expect the world to "bow" to our influence, regardless of the quality of that influence. The truth is, we're competing with other influencers for the hearts and minds of our society, and this requires that we make every effort to win the battle of influence. We need not imitate secular, cultural influencers; we need only present the good news of the kingdom with all of the passion, vitality, quality, and excellence that we can muster, through the power of the Holy Spirit and to the glory of our God.